OMNIVM
LVX
CIVIVM
MDCCCLII
MDCCC
LXXVIII
BOSTON
PUBLIC
LIBRARY

Published by Golf Digest/Tennis, Inc., a New York Times Company, 495 Westport Avenue, P.O. Box 5350, Norwalk, Connecticut 06856

Trade book distribution by Simon and Schuster, A Division of Gulf + Western Industries, Inc. New York, New York 10020

ISBN: 0-914178-53-9
Library of Congress: 83-81075
Manufactured in the United States of America

Photo and Art Credits

Cover illustration by Walter Einsel; Walter Einsel: p. 9; William C. Brooks: p. 11; Melchior DiGiacomo: pp. 14, 121; Stephen Szurlej: pp. 6, 11, 13, 17, 21, 29, 46-47, 61, 63, 65, 69, 71, 75, 85, 91-92, 93, 94-95, 111, 113, 133, 135, 137; Ronald L. Mrowiec: p. 20; Art Seitz: pp. 34-35, 36, 57, 147; John Crowther: p. 45; Elmer Wexler: pp. 53, 55, 58-59, 62, 64, 67, 68, 79, 97, 99, 101, 103, 105; Dick Kohfield: pp. 76-77, 79; Ron Galella: p. 115; Wide World Photos: pp. 119, 157; Russ Adams Productions: pp. 125, 129; USTA: p. 143; Larry Petrillo: p. 150; Conrad Studios: p. 153.

Cover and book design
by Michael Brent,
Graphics Director—
Golf Digest/Tennis Inc.

The Tennis Grand Masters:
HOW TO PLAY WINNING TENNIS IN THE PRIME OF LIFE

Acknowledgments

Special thanks to Drummond C. Bell, the Chairman of the Board of National Distillers & Chemical Corp.; to the International Management Group, current proprietors of the Tennis Grand Masters circuit; and to Robert J. LaMarche, Associate Editor of TENNIS magazine.

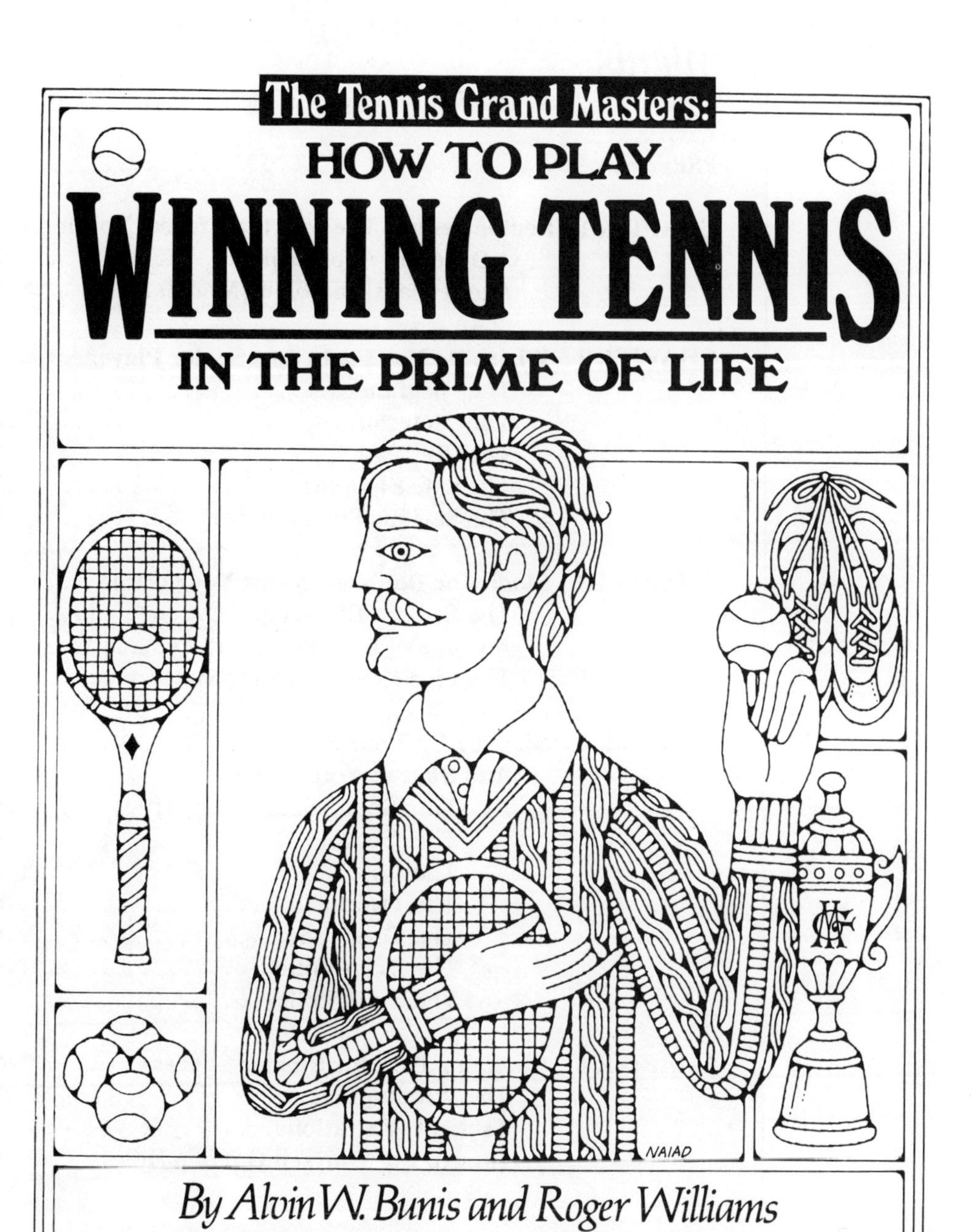
The Tennis Grand Masters:
HOW TO PLAY
WINNING TENNIS
IN THE PRIME OF LIFE
NAIAD
By Alvin W. Bunis and Roger Williams

Contents

PREFACE **4**

CHAPTER 1 **Senior Tennis: The Sport of Eternal Youth** **9**
A Different Approach **12**
Adopt Classic Stroking Models **16**

CHAPTER 2 **Where Do You Fit In As a Senior Player?** **23**
The Beginner **24**
The Veteran **27**
The Retread **30**
The Late Bloomer **37**
The Serious Social Player **39**

CHAPTER 3 **Singles or Doubles? Name Your Game** **43**
The Stiffest Challenge **44**
A Game of Complex Strategy **48**
The Five Keys to Senior Success **49**

CHAPTER 4 **Shoring Up Your Strokes** **51**
Add Spin to Your Game **52**
Re-Think Shot Selection Priorities **56**
The Serve **56**
The Lob **60**
The Overhead **62**
The Drop Shot **65**
The Drop Volley **68**
The Half Volley **70**

CHAPTER 5 **Changing Pace for Singles Success** **73**
The Winning Basics **74**
Tactical Variations **76**
How to Dig Yourself Out of a Hole **82**

CHAPTER 6 Winning With Opportunistic Doubles 89
Offensive Tactics 92
The Importance of Teamwork 92
Exploit Your Serving Advantage 98
Blunt the Server's Edge 102

CHAPTER 7 Using Your Head to Win 109
Concentrate for a Psychological Lift 110
Your Invisible Weapon 112

CHAPTER 8 Conditioning Your Body to Perform 117
General Fitness 120
Pre-Match Stretching Routines 126

CHAPTER 9 Coming Back From Injuries and Layoffs 131
Remarkable Comebacks 134
Coming Back After a Layoff 138

CHAPTER 10 Getting Better As You Get Older 141
Use Practice Time Wisely 144
Seek Professional Assistance 148
Check Out The Latest Equipment 149
Racquets 149
Stringing 152
Footwear 153

CHAPTER 11 Testing the Tournament Waters 155
Match Preparation 156
Match Play 160

Authors' Preface

Right now, you're probably asking yourself, "What's this? Another book on tennis?"

Well, yes and no. Yes, this is a book on tennis. But no, it is not *just* another one. This book addresses a select and rapidly growing segment of the world's tennis-playing population: competitors in the middle-age bracket.

Is that worth a book in itself? It certainly is, and the following 11 chapters will tell you why. Tennis is one of the few vigorous, competitive physical activities that can be pursued into middle age and beyond. But—and here's the crux of our thesis—it is a sport that demands of its successful practitioners some concessions.

These concessions involve attitude and approach, both on and off the court. They involve strokes, strategy, psychology, conditioning and, above all, a realistic assessment of one's own abilities, limitations, and attitudes.

If that sounds like a prescription for a genteel game of old men's (or old ladies') pat-ball, be assured that it is not. Tennis at middle age can be as fast-moving and hard-hitting as you're able to make it.

As living proof, we offer active, exemplary competitors: the touring players of the Tennis Grand Masters circuit. The Grand Masters are former world-class players, 45 years of age or over, who have been competing against each other in tournaments all over the world since 1973. Their ranks have included many of the great names in tennis history: Frank Sedgman, Pancho Gonzalez, Roy Emerson, Vic Seixas, Neale Fraser, Frank Parker, Pancho Segura, Bobby Riggs, Gardnar Mulloy, Don Budge, Alex Olmedo, and others too numerous to mention.

In part, it was the inception of the Grand Masters circuit some 10 years ago that helped focus national attention on senior competition and trigger the present-day surge in organized events for the maturing player. The tour provided a stage upon which the Grand Masters could showcase their still-exceptional stroking and playing skills. Sure, the veterans may have lacked a step or two of quickness they owned in their primes, but they served as an inspiration to amateur senior players to continue competing and, in many cases, come out of retirement.

In essence, these men have proved for the first time in any physically demanding sport, that stylish, competitive, interesting spectator tennis can be played well past your prime—*if* you're willing to make the necessary mental and physical preparations as well as the elemental concessions mentioned above. For this reason, the experiences, techniques and observations of the Grand Masters form the backbone of this book. They are middle-aged tennis players and so are you. We're confident you'll find that you have, or could have, a great deal in common.

Introducing the authors:

Alvin W. Bunis, 59, a Cincinnatian, brings an encyclopedic knowledge of the senior game to bear in *The Tennis Grand Masters: How to Play Winning Tennis in the Prime of Life.* As a player, he has attained national rankings in both junior and senior play; as an instructor, he has conducted hundreds of tennis clinics and thus, has come to know the needs and frustrations of beginners and intermediate players.

Bunis, who compiles and determines the only rankings of the world's senior players, also founded and directed the Tennis Grand Masters tour. In this capacity, he estimates that he has viewed more than 2,000 matches, played by some of the greatest players in the history of tennis. His vast experience forms the basis of his conclusions about how to play the senior game.

Roger Williams, 50, a freelance writer based in New York City, has played at the "A" level since his teenage days as a member of the Westchester County (N.Y.) Junior Davis Cup team. Although Williams still enters an occasional tournament, he plays what he calls "serious social" tennis. That is, he stays in shape and frequently works to improve his game.

Senior Tennis: The Sport of Eternal Youth

In the past, it seems, most tennis players gave up the sport in their 40s or 50s. The belief was that tennis was too strenuous, perhaps too life-threatening, to be played regularly and vigorously at middle age and beyond. Instead of tennis, a man or woman often took up golf—a fine game, but hardly a taxing one physically.

All that has changed dramatically in the last decade. It is common these days to meet people who've *taken up* tennis in their 40s or 50s. And it has become increasingly rare to meet anybody who's *given it up* at that age.

C. Alphonso Smith, 73, one of the principal organizers of today's "Super Senior" competition, estimates that in the swelling ranks of today's senior players, "a very large number have taken up tennis in the past 10 years. Maybe they played as kids and then turned to golf. Now, doctors are telling their patients in golf carts, 'Hey, you're not getting enough exercise,' so they're getting out and playing tennis a couple of times a week."

Although statistical proof is sketchy, tennis authorities agree that the sport has been enjoying its most rapid growth at the senior level. Tournament statistics show the degree to which competitive play has increased. According to the United States Tennis Association (USTA), the number of sanctioned tournaments in the 35-and-over age division doubled between 1970 and 1980—from 65 to 130. During that same decade, the number of sanctioned events in the 60-and-over categories surpassed 200. And there are now national championships for 80-year-olds. That's right—80-year-olds.

Indeed, the growth in so-called Super Senior tournaments—for ages 55 through 75, in five-year increments—has been little short of amazing. Formed in 1973, the Super Seniors organization has already enrolled 2,500 members who contribute a minimum of $10 a year and play in one or more of the dozens of tournaments run by the group. Says Smith: "People talk about how tennis has leveled off, but *our* catagory of tennis is growing all the time. We play national championships on all four surfaces in each division. In Florida, between January and mid-March, you can play

Frank Sedgman: playing "the big game" as a Grand Master.

a Super Senior tournament every week if you want to."

The seniors are thriving in women's competition as well. "Several years ago, the women wouldn't even admit they *were* 40 or 50," chuckles Dorothy "Dodo" Cheney, the seemingly ageless champion from southern California. "Now they're saying, 'Great—next year I'll be eligible to play in the 50's!' And 20 years ago, nobody even thought of a tournament for 55-year-old women. Now we've got 'em for 70-and-over."

Mature folks' tournament tennis has even developed media sex appeal, a sure sign of popular success. During recent years, Super Seniors championships have been covered by network television.

But tournaments aren't the only indicators of the growth of senior tennis. There's also plenty of everyday evidence. For example, there's the popularity of the tennis clinics taught in conjunction with the Grand Masters tour; the tennis chatter that inevitably surfaces at cocktail parties, PTA meetings, business conventions, everywhere that middle-aged players gather; the terrific sales of oversized racquets, which initially were developed and marketed for the middle-aged player; the onset of a complete tennis fashion industry, aimed at the more affluent and generally older player; and the best evidence of all, the profusion of gray and/or balding heads seen on courts—public and private, hard and soft—from New York to California.

A DIFFERENT APPROACH

Whether you're barely 45 or at the upper end of the Super Seniors age bracket, a fiercely competitive tournament player or a genial weekend hacker, tennis at your age should be treated as a special game. It is not the tennis of youth, which depends so much on speed afoot, powerful strokes, and strength instead of finesse. It is, rather, a game of patience, placement, positioning, stamina, and what tennis players call consistency or steadiness—the ability to keep the ball in play rather than try for lower-percentage winning shots. It is essentially a backcourt game because rushing the net repeatedly requires lots of energy, and winning points once you're there requires quick reflexes and probably a forceful, accurate overhead smash.

Neale Fraser: attacking the ball at every opportunity.

There are, of course, exceptions: middle-aged players who hit with consistent "pace," cover the net adroitly, and win with something resembling what used to be called "the big game"—hard serves, deep approach shots and crunching volleys. The Grand Masters circuit boasts the best of these players, among them Frank Sedgman, Roy Emerson, Neale Fraser, Mal Anderson, Alex Olmedo and Fred Stolle.

Olmedo, 47, serves at least as hard now as he did when he was a U.S. Davis Cup star in the late 1950s. Fraser, 49, doesn't serve quite as hard as he did in his prime—he had one of the fastest serves tennis has ever known—but it is still a great weapon against any opponent and Fraser capitalizes with it at every opportunity. Anderson, a trim and agile 48, displays an all-court game worthy of an international-class player half his age.

At 55, Sedgman plays the judiciously aggressive game that has earned him the Grand Masters singles championship six of the 10 years the title has been contested. The truly remarkable part of his game is the volley. He is perhaps the finest volleyer of all time, and he still relies heavily on assuming command in the forecourt, essentially the domain of a younger man, to win the key points.

Sedgman serves as the perfect example of how extraordinary athletic ability can be preserved well into middle age. He makes as little concession to advancing years as anyone ever has in the history of tennis. Conceding six, seven, eight years to some of his Grand Masters opponents, all of them first-class players, he frequently comes away the victor.

But—and it's a very large but—there's only one Sedgman, and darnned few Frasers, Olmedos and Andersons. Their use of power and attacking techniques cannot serve the rest of us middle-agers as models. For that, and for something approaching practical instruction, we must turn to other, less-flamboyant parts of the Grand Masters' games: the depth and angles with which they hit their ground strokes; their deft use of the drop shot and lob; the consistency and placement of their second serves; their anticipation; and finally, their economy of movement and

Roy Emerson: still rushing the net after all these years.

ability to pace themselves through the course of a long, tiring match.

Those are the winning strokes and stratagems that can make the average middle-aged player's game more effective. Indeed, Cliff Drysdale, a fortyish former international star, says, "It's much easier to learn from watching the Grand Masters than the guys on the regular circuit. The younger fellows are too fast, and their game is a bit far removed from what the average player is able to do. The Grand Masters are more classical, and you can really see what they are doing."

Not long ago, Sedgman himself noted: "We've found that people who've taken up tennis in the last few years can relate to us better than to (Bjorn) Borg, (John) McEnroe and (Jimmy) Connors. And they can see how *they* can play a pretty high-level game in their middle years."

ADOPT CLASSIC STROKING MODELS

Both Drysdale and Sedgman make an important point: the average player, whatever his age, has little to learn by watching the form of today's young champions. Not only are they too speedy, powerful, and talented, most of them are also too unorthodox. Who can emulate Borg's two-handed backhand, the exaggerated topspin of Guillermo Vilas, the jerky but tremendous serve of McEnroe? Whatever its advantages and attractions, the contemporary game at the highest level has become far too wristy, too Ping-Pong-like, to be instructive to anyone, save an occasional supremely-talented youngster.

The best seniors, on the other hand, all play one or another version of what Drysdale aptly calls the classical game. The critical differences are found in the ground strokes. In the classical game, going back to the days of the legendary Bill Tilden, they are smooth and flowing. The backswing is early, the weight transfers from back foot to front as the racquet moves forward, and the stroke, slightly upward and "over" the ball, finishes with a long follow-through. There are variations, of course, such as the underspin backhand, but even the variations bear far greater resemblance to the classical strokes than to those perfected by Borg,

Mal Anderson: displaying an all-court game in middle age.

McEnroe, and their rivals.

So there's still a lot you can learn by studying the classical games of the Grand Masters. And remember this: You *can* improve—whatever your level of play—at middle age. There's no need to think that, at 45 or 55, you're struggling to maintain a holding pattern, merely keeping your game from slipping.

In our tennis lifetimes, we've both seen many examples of players who've realized substantial improvement even after they supposedly passed their prime. Consider the cases of two Grand Masters: one who now plays better than in his first several years on the circuit, and the other who, in the opinions of many observers, plays better than he did 25 years ago.

The first man is Fraser, whose Grand Masters performance has improved considerably since he strengthened his backhand. In his Davis Cup days, playing primarily on fast surfaces where his booming serves exacted a harsh toll on opponents, Fraser was able to win without a big-league backhand. His other shots—forehands, volleys, overheads, and especially serves—more than made up for his relatively weak backhand. When he entered the Grand Masters circuit and began playing on slower courts with a less-powerful serve, however, he found that his opponents, all skillful ground-strokers, could exploit his backhand.

Fraser's answer was not to curse the fates or quit the Grand Masters, but to work on his backhand. His approach was not a matter of mechanics—that is, of changing his stroke—but of practice. He hit thousands of practice backhands. And he used the slow courts to his own advantage, taking more time to prepare for the stroke and to hit "through" the ball. Bit by bit, the Fraser backhand, honed in the man's late 40s, became a weapon, producing a strong approach shot here, a crackling passing shot there.

The other "improved" Grand Master is Torben Ulrich, the bearded, poetic, jazz-loving Dane. It's fruitless to ask Torben if *he* thinks he's playing better now than in years past. Forever philosophical, he will smile beatifically and reply, "Don't you think that depends on what one considers 'better'?"

Alex Olmedo: using quick reflexes to cut off passing shots.

Fred Stolle: taking command of a point from the forecourt.

Those who do think he's a stronger player today point to a developing topspin backhand as the main reason. Heavy topspin is not something one ordinarily adds to a backhand in middle age; it's pretty much the province of young people learning the sport. But Ulrich spends a lot of time pondering his game, practically as well as metaphysically, and he calculated the value of topspin: First, there's the high bounce near the baseline that keeps opponents on the defensive, then there's the dipping ball, so difficult to volley by net rushers. Topspin also gave him the ability to suddenly change pace against all those classic strokers in the Grand Masters, and, not least for him, the opportunity to master a new aspect of the sport to which he's devoted

Torben Ulrich: always looking for ways to improve his game.

four decades of his life. A cautious man on the court, Ulrich is gradually trying to make the topspin backhand an effective weapon in his stroking arsenal.

Can your own game accommodate topspin? Do you have the stamina and reflexes, not to mention the shots, to take the net repeatedly? Or should you rely on the standard middle-age strategy of playing with steadiness and patience from the backcourt, with a few well-timed changes of pace thrown in?

The answers to those questions will go a long way toward determining what you put into and get out of tennis at middle age. We'll deal with them in detail, starting with the next chapter that asks the most basic question of all: What kind of player are you?

Where Do You Fit In As a Senior Player?

When you take up a physically demanding sport in youth, your concerns are relatively simple. First, you determine how much you like the game. Then, you budget your time to it accordingly. But when you take up a sport in middle age, things become a bit more complicated. Lifestyle and family considerations, for example, enter the picture. You have to ask yourself: "How much time *can* I devote to tennis? Can I become good enough to really enjoy it? Do I want to do the practicing and the physical conditioning needed to achieve a measure of competitive success?"

As we've already indicated, the last of those questions requires a lot of thought and a sense of one's own desires and limitations. The first two, however, can be answered easily. Tennis does require a commitment of time and money, but almost anyone can become good enough to enjoy playing.

That covers beginners. But there are other categories of middle-aged players, too: veterans, who've gone at it several times a week for years; "retreads," who gave up the game and want to resume it; "late bloomers," who are determined to upgrade the level of their play; and finally, serious social players, who enjoy tough competition, but not necessarily in a tournament format.

We'll discuss these categories in sequence, according to how experienced and how serious their members are. You'll find that placing yourself in a category may not be as simple as you'd think, that it can involve psychological, as well as physical considerations. You'll also find, as we cite cases from our personal tennis experiences, that so-called average players can become dramatically better.

THE BEGINNER

If you can run, even a little, you're not too old to begin playing tennis. Take Peg South of Laguna Beach, California. She was 66 when she retired as a gift shop owner and took up the sport. At last report, she was 83 and a regular member of her local club's "B" team. What's more, on two occasions, she's toured overseas with People-to-People tennis groups sponsored by the U.S. Department of State.

Most middle-aged beginners will get started in their 40s or early 50s. Whatever the age, with a sensible approach and a modicum of ability, you can develop into a creditable player in about six months.

The first step in starting to play tennis at middle age is a precautionary one: a visit to your physician. Unless you've been jogging or playing racquetball or a comparable sport, tennis is going to subject your body to unaccustomed stresses and strains. Chances are they'll prove no problem for you, but a doctor's checkup is the surest way to find out. The checkup will measure your pulse, blood pressure, and weight, the last to make sure you won't be overloading your heart by hauling too many pounds around the court. It should also include a review of past or present ailments that might be aggravated by strenuous exercise.

Observes Dr. James A. Nicholas, a renowned practitioner of sports medicine: "Anyone who's going to start an activity like tennis should first calculate the level, intensity, and duration of his intended play. If you've had trouble with your back or knees or shoulder—all of which are common by middle age—you should acknowledge that and prepare for it." There is a tendency, he adds, for overweight people to turn to sports like tennis in order to "get back into shape." Without the proper medical counsel and precautions, that can be dangerous.

Dr. Nicholas, who directs New York City's Institute of Sports Medicine and serves as orthopedic consultant to the professional Jets (football), Rangers (hockey), Knicks (basketball), and Cosmos (soccer), recommends that anyone taking up tennis past the age of 35 submit to a physical examination that tests three vital areas: cardiovascular fitness, muscular structure, and your body's general ability to respond to what doctors call the "cumulative impact loading" of strenuous activity in hot weather.

A sports-medicine specialist is the best person to see for such matters, but that specialty is not yet widespread. Next best, according to Dr. Nicholas, is an orthopedist: "He treats the parts of the body—joints, muscles, bones—that are most likely to give tennis players problems." And if, for some reason, an orthopedist isn't available, it's O.K. to start with your family practitioner. He knows your health history and the basic indicators to check in behalf of a beginning player.

Dr. Nicholas cautions: "I would *not*, however, get the job done by anyone with a nonscientific background—a physical therapist, fitness evaluator, chiropractor, or guru in matters of fitness. Although they may have been made somewhat proficient by exposure to sports-related ailments, they should not be entrusted with this kind of screening."

Assuming you're physically fit, you're ready to learn how to hit a tennis ball. Perhaps a friend or your husband or wife can teach you. But beware, spouses tend to make about as suitable teaching pros as they do bridge partners. So don't be surprised if both teacher and pupil wind up frustrated and angry after a couple of lessons. Your best bet probably will be to hire a tennis professional. He can introduce you to the game and the mechanics of its basic strokes, and can do so with a patience and emotional detachment that people close to you cannot match.

And while you're setting aside time for lessons, don't forget to add time for practicing what you'll learn. Lessons without regular and continuous practice have little value. Learning to play tennis is a matter of "grooving" your strokes. This requires constant repetition of the correct backswing, swing, and follow-through—at first in an almost stationary position, then on the move, the way you'll be doing it in actual play.

You should begin playing sets as soon as possible, however. All practice and no play makes for a mighty dull game; the fun of tennis lies in the competition, not in hitting balls. When you can get half your serves in the court and hit three balls in succession over the net, you should start keeping score. You'll soon find out what every player before you has discovered: that it's a lot easier to hit balls well when a pro is "laying them on your racquet" than when an opponent is trying his best to keep you from making returns. When you're forced to run, change direction, hit balls of varying speeds, and think about what's coming next, you are really playing tennis.

Don't expect consistent, picture-perfect strokes when you play sets. You will inevitably sacrifice some of your newly learned techniques to the expediency of winning points. That's not all bad. You'll always need to be able to improvise slightly on what you've learned. Anyway, in match play even at high levels, very few balls are hit in textbook fashion.

Should you learn the game on one particular surface? We recommend learning on an all-weather, "hard" court if possible. The bounce on this surface is uniform and true, compared to the uncertainties of the soft-court bounce. It is also somewhat faster which will force you to move your feet nimbly and get your racquet back early—keys to hitting the ball well. Furthermore, since you can't slide on a hard surface as on clay, you'll avoid some of the habits of sloppy footwork that even good clay-court players develop.

Finally, as a middle-aged beginner, remember that you have one advantage over your younger counterparts—emotional and intellectual maturity that should help you analyze and reflect on your game.

THE VETERAN

At some point in middle age, the experienced, longtime player is going to begin to lose whatever has been the foundation of his game: the ability to take the net decisively, to run all day in the backcourt or to win five or six points a set outright with the first serve. Call it the tennis player's "law of inevitability." The onset and rapidity of the loss will vary with different players, of course, depending on general physical condition and on such specific physical factors as speed afoot, muscle tone, and hand-eye coordination.

To continue to play at the peak of his ability, the veteran has to make adjustments. In broadest terms, they require replacing power, speed and stamina with consistency, wise court positioning and guile.

Some players, to be sure, make few concessions of

this sort. They stick with "their game" like a captain and his slowly sinking ship. Only poor or very good players can succeed with this approach. In the second group, Frank Sedgman stands out. Sedgman remains basically a serve-and-volley player. Of course, he has less power and speed than he did as a Wimbledon champion, but so do his opponents.

If Sedgman has made any age-directed change, it is in volleying position. He no longer gets in so close to the net and often can be found volleying around the service line. In tennis parlance, that area, particularly behind the service line, is "no-man's land," and one of the enduring tactical rules is never to get caught there. But a volleyer of Sedgman's caliber handles no-man's land with ease. The fact that he can play effectively there enables him to take fewer steps when advancing to the net.

We mortal volleyers can't get away with that. If we stop in no-man's land, we get too many low balls we can't handle; and even if we can handle them, we're unable to put our volleys away. Our options are to go to the net less frequently or behind shots that are hit from an area *closer* to the net. That is typical of the middle-age adjustments mentioned above.

Yet adjustment need not mean cutting back on using a tactic or maneuver that you used to perform well. It can, and should, mean *adding* dimensions to your game: for instance, new or improved strokes. The drop shot, a punishing weapon in senior tennis, is an obvious example.

There are psychological, as well as set-winning, benefits to this type of improvement. Who better to describe them than Torben Ulrich, the court philosopher?

"Even if you're declining physically," says Ulrich, "there can be growth in the wholeness of your game. You can be slicing under the ball with one shot, coming over it with the next. Or you can be trying the attacking lob, seeing if that kind of shot can be developed at your age." In Ulrich's case, it's been the development of a topspin backhand and topspin backhand lob that has paid off. He happily recalls his first triumphant use of

Super veteran: Sedgman defies tennis' "law of inevitability."

the lob: "It was in the Grand Masters' Hawaii tournament last summer, against (Neale) Fraser. I hit one on match point, and it worked." For a tennis player of Ulrich's age, at any level, that is a memorable, satisfying experience.

THE RETREAD

The comeback player is often one who was quite accomplished in his first tennis life. Former tournament players who got tired of the pressure and the practice make up a sizable segment of this category. So do A- or B-level players who gave up the game in the face of business or family obligations. Now, usually because of a desire to stay physically fit, they want to return to tennis.

Our award for greatest comeback would go to former Grand Master Rex Hartwig. An Australian Davis Cup star and one of history's finest doubles players, Hartwig dropped off the tournament circuit in 1959 to settle down to an active ranch life in Greta, Victoria. For the next 17—yes, 17—years, he hardly touched a racquet and never hit a ball in earnest. Then, midway through the Grand Masters' 1976 tour, he was asked to fill out the field for a tournament in Sydney, Australia. With a few days' practice, he took to the courts and played himself into the finals, where he held a match point against Sedgman before going down in defeat!

The retread player should keep two things in mind. The first is his physical condition. Unless he's kept himself in shape in the interim years, he is a beginner from a medical standpoint and will need the beginner's checkup. The second involves mental attitude and it can be very difficult to resolve. There is only a limited relationship between the way any retread used to play and the way he can play now. Former champions will quickly discover that their credentials and memories of how to hit a ball often will not take them far in senior play.

Their diminished skills, of course, contribute to this situation. But so does the presence in the senior ranks of lots of new faces, people who were mediocre players—or even non-players—in youth, but who have

Retread extraordinaire: Rex Hartwig came back in style.

been working hard at their games during those years when the retread didn't go near a court.

In this sense, age is a great leveler in tennis. Nobodies become somebodies in the senior game, often at the expense of former somebodies who simply aren't what they used to be.

If you were once a fine player, this raises an interesting and potentially troublesome question: Are you willing to risk losing to players whom you could have beaten, maybe even *did* beat, easily way back when? The top ranks of today's seniors are well supplied with people who've answered the question both ways.

Dick Savitt, a former Wimbledon and Australian champion, has in effect said "no." Savitt, a New York City businessman who still plays regularly and very well, has been eligible to compete on the Grand Masters circuit for several years, but he has not done so. He prefers to keep his tennis on the serious social level.

Other ex-champions have chosen to stay out of the competitive limelight as well. One is Tony Trabert, who quit at the young age of 33. "When I retired," Trabert said a few years ago, "I decided that I was simply unwilling to pay the price physically and mentally anymore." Now a TV commentator and the director of a successful children's tennis camp in California, he has never felt the need to get back into shape and join his former rivals among the Grand Masters.

Many of those who did join the circuit have restricted their competitive activity to that rarified level. For one thing, they would have to seek permission to play in a non-Grand Masters event. But there is a more personal reason: an unwillingness to risk their reputations against relative nobodies. Explains Vic Seixas, one of the premier players of the post-War era: "Every time you go out on the court against a local player, it's a no-win situation. If you lose, you're a bum, and if you win, so what?"

In the early years of the Grand Masters, Seixas made no secret of his displeasure at losing to Ulrich and Sven Davidson, who had been world-class competitors but hardly titans of the sport. (Ulrich often jokes that he lost more Davis Cup matches, playing for Denmark, than anyone else in history.) Age can be a capricious mistress to tennis players. She afflicted Seixas with troublesome arthritis while blessing Ulrich with excellent health and the suppleness of a 25-year-old.

Consider, however, Gardnar Mulloy and Bobby Riggs, two former greats who have competed relentlessly in senior championships below the Grand Masters level. Mulloy, now a magnificent 69, dominated the senior scene for years with only a few bad losses. As John McEnroe and Bjorn Borg can testify, you can't play tournament after tournament without an occasional bad loss. But if there is a Seixas-type of pride which keeps that former star from risking blemishes on his record, there is also a Mulloy type. "Gar" is justly proud of his physical condition and the tennis skills he's retained. Beyond that, he loves to play this game on a competitive basis.

Nobody, though, loves competition more than Riggs. He'll go almost anywhere to play almost anybody if he considers it worthwhile. Riggs' use of the adjective "worthwhile," people often say, pertains to the amount of money at stake in a match in prizes and side bets. Certainly, Riggs likes the money; he's an inveterate bettor. But anyone who thinks he plays for that reason alone simply doesn't know the man. They don't realize how many tournaments he's played in where there was little or no money to be won.

Along the way—and this is the real point about Riggs—he's suffered losses that others with far slimmer credentials might have considered humiliating. Riggs, bear in mind, was not only the best player of *his* time; he was one of the best of *all* time. Yet he has lost tournament matches, in recent years, to such players as Buck Archer and Ken Wilson, whose names not one percent of the readers of this book will recognize.

But those are the hazards of senior tennis, and Riggs has the guts and the personality to accept them. "When you're young and you've been programmed to be a champ," he said recently, "you win because it's expected of you. Now, you realize you're not as fast and you gotta make a bigger effort. Hey, I remember when they couldn't hit a ball by me. Not anymore. But that's O.K. It's still good competition and I get just as big a kick out of winning a tough match now as I did then."

What about his former peers who won't "risk it" as seniors? "I don't have a lot of respect for guys like that," replies Riggs, forever straightforward with his opinions. "I'm disappointed in Savitt and Trabert. This business about protecting your record is ridiculous. We're *in* the record book; nobody can take our records away. Look at Bill Tilden. He kept playing right into his 60s. I played him when he was an old man and beat

Bobby Riggs on senior competition: "I get just as big a kick out of winning a tough match now as I did then."

him, and he never said anything like, 'When I was in my prime, I woulda clobbered you.' He played for all he was worth and had some phenomenally good wins when he was well along in years."

Now 65, Riggs has lost his top ranking in the national 60's division to Bob Sherman. But even if he drops lower than that, he insists he won't stop competing: "I enjoy the winning, sure, but as long as I'm a contender

in my division, I'm gonna stay with it. Anyway, I still think I'm gonna win everytime I step onto the court."

This kind of perseverance has its own price. The public has come to think of Riggs as a funny little guy who clowns his way through matches and can be blown away by any reasonably accomplished opponent. The much-ballyhooed loss to Billie Jean King, together with Riggs' appetite for extravagant and sometimes tasteless publicity, have reinforced that impression. But there is another Riggs—the tough match player with a still-stunning array of shots, the graceful loser with a cheerful word to his conqueror, however obscure the man—or woman—may be.

Wilson was one of those obscure conquerors a few years ago. A lanky and genial fellow from southern New Jersey, Wilson defeated Riggs—several years his elder—in the 55's division of the national grass courts championship, winning the last 11 games of the match. Sudden adversity of that sort would turn many a tournament favorite into a sullen loser, but not Riggs. "He was very gracious about it," Wilson recalls. "No disparaging remarks or excuses. What struck me was his willingness to risk his record like that. He's the consummate competitor."

THE LATE BLOOMER

Because tennis is a lifelong sport with competitive play available along the entire route, different faces pop up time and again. The junior champion may never be heard from again; the finalist in the 55's may be somebody who never used to get past the first round. (In this respect, C. Alphonso Smith, the Super Seniors organizer, has a matchless record. Smith boasts a spread of 55 years between national championships. He won the national boys' singles and doubles in 1924 and the national 70's hardcourt doubles in 1979. He hopes to extend the spread even further.) All this adds variety to the sport, and, unlike virtually every other com-

Senior pride: Gardnar Mulloy (left), a trim and agile 69, put his playing record on the line for years with only a few bad losses.

petitive activity, it brings eminence within the reach of a good many people.

In each division of senior play, you'll find several spots in the top-10 rankings held by players who were not of national caliber in their youth. Many of them played tennis then only casually or not at all. A good example is Sherman, the Californian who took the number one spot in the 60's away from Riggs in 1980 and has held onto the top ranking ever since. Sherman was a star athlete at the University of Southern California but he played little tennis until he committed himself to the game in his 30s.

Atlantan Charlie Kidd came out of nowhere to capture the number one senior ranking in the South in 1980. Ten years ago, Kidd was, by his own admission, shunned by the good players at Atlanta's Bitsy Grant Tennis Center. Now, he has the pleasure of beating those same players . . . whenever he can lure them onto the court.

Kidd attributes his success to good conditioning, athletic ability, and above all, determination: "I enjoyed the game before, but never got serious about it. I never cared about being good." Finishing as runner-up in the Georgia Indoors a few years ago convinced him that he could indeed be good, and he's been playing with a purpose ever since—five or six times a week, twice as much singles play as doubles.

Wilson has played for many years, but his game has improved markedly in the past decade. (He ranked in the top 20 nationally in the 45's and remains one of the best seniors in the Middle Atlantic area.) "Success at this age," he says, "is a function of the patterns of maturation. The differences in how people age level out the differences in ability. I've improved, basically, because my physical condition's remained satisfactory. I haven't had a weight problem or serious ailments."

Our prize exhibits in the late-bloomer category, Ray Murphy and Ken Matthews, should be an inspiration to every also-ran approaching middle age. Murphy, 60, and Matthews, 59, are residents of Cincinnati. As a doubles team, they have emerged from obscurity to become one of the best 55-and-over combinations in the country. In 1980, they ranked fourth.

By several measures, the two are quite dissimilar. Matthews, a strapping six-footer, likes to play singles and to spend time in practice sessions. He takes lessons periodically. Murphy, slight and wiry, plays no singles and never practices. He takes no lessons. ("I took some when I began playing, but I realized my limitations and stopped.")

Where they come together is in their fierce desire to improve and in their unorthodox, but highly effective style of doubles play. That style—based entirely on offense—is built around Murphy's remarkable game. As he himself cheerfully admits, he has no shots that would be thought of as conventional ground strokes. His serve does little more than put the ball in play, and on the service return, he either lobs or blocks the ball back low. To say he rushes the net is an understatement—he swarms over it, constantly, relying on superb reflexes to handle whatever the opponents fire at him.

Both men have been playing tennis for 15 to 20 years. Not until they joined forces and made improvement a top priority, however, did they begin to win regularly in tournaments. "It's a real satisfaction beating people who've played the game well for years," Matthews says. "Especially people who laugh when they see us warming up." Murphy agrees that because he can't rally in the standard fashion, "the warm-up period sometimes gets a little tense. The guy opposite me wants to hit from the baseline, but I can't get more than a couple of balls in a row over the net from there." Anyway, he adds with a chuckle, "I'm not gonna let him practice his ground strokes when I don't have any to practice."

In the manner typical of late bloomers, Murphy and Matthews look forward to, not backward at, tennis achievements. "We're anxious to get into the 60's division," Murphy says. "We'll be better, and the other guys won't be as good."

THE SERIOUS SOCIAL PLAYER

If you're serious about your tennis—and because you're reading this book, you probably are—you have to decide at some point whether you want to play in tournaments—that is, play in them on a fairly regular basis.

For the kinds of players we've discussed thus far, the decision is easier. But it is not necessarily so for the rest of us. Tournament play demands commitments in time and effort and carries the built-in risk of "public" failure. Some people habitually play poorly in tournaments and are more likely to come away from them feeling frustrated than fulfilled. And let's face it, few of us middle-agers want to expose ourselves to avoidable frustrations.

In addition, not many of us want to devote the time and attention that tournaments require. When you add up the hours spent traveling to events and waiting for your matches, you realize what tournament tennis, played regularly, demands.

In middle age, that kind of singleness of purpose is very difficult to sustain. When you play a bunch of senior tournaments, you might suddenly think, "What am I doing, consumed like this at my age? I've got a business to run and a family to support and be part of." You can't avoid feeling guilty.

Fortunately, participation in tournaments is not an essential ingredient for serious and satisfying tennis. The only essential ingredient is caring about your game, which translates into selecting suitably tough opponents, playing your best against them, and carving *enough* time from your schedule to make tennis a major activity. Depending on your own goals and temperament, it can also translate into taking lessons and practicing.

Here are a couple of qualifications you should consider in choosing opponents: In both style and caliber of play, they should be a varied group. Playing against different styles will keep your game from settling into too deep a rut. As for level of play, if your opponents are always too tough, you'll never get a chance to play your good shots; if they're always too weak, you won't get a chance to work on the defensive part of your game.

And finally, if your playing time is limited, stay away from opponents who can't be depended on to try hard when they're not playing up to par. Everyone has bad days, but to give up and simply go through the motions is a discourtesy—to say the least—to the person across the net.

Singles or Doubles? Name Your Game

Very few sports offer their participants alternative forms of play. Tennis is one of the exceptions. The sport encompasses two games that share the same basic principles, yet differ considerably in terms of style of play, shots and physical exertion required. Which one should you choose—singles or doubles? Since the great majority of people *can* play both, perhaps the better question is: Which one should you emphasize?

Our unequivocal answer, for those who are physically able, is singles. As far as we're concerned, singles is *the* game. Doubles is merely an entertaining, challenging sideshow. Why should singles be top-rated? Because it alone rewards the player who has stayed in good physical condition and has developed an all-around game.

Doubles, on the other hand, accommodates those who are much less than physically fit and whose repertoires of shots contain gaping holes. Hence, the rise of the doubles "specialist." We're not trying to denigrate these people or their styles of play, but simply to point out that singles is the truer test in tennis. The sport's spectators recognize this fact and, therefore, so do its promoters. Compare the amounts of prize money they put up for singles or doubles. Today's leading singles players are millionaires, while the leading doubles players are. . . very good doubles players.

THE STIFFEST CHALLENGE

Having pounded home that opinion, we want to point out that each game has natural appeal to players with quite different objectives. Singles is the obvious choice for those who want exercise, and the stiffest test when it comes to endurance under match pressure. Nothing short of two hours of high-level doubles will provide a

A demanding game: Singles play is the tennis version of bullfighting's "mano a mano." It's just you and your opponent out there on opposite sides of the net.

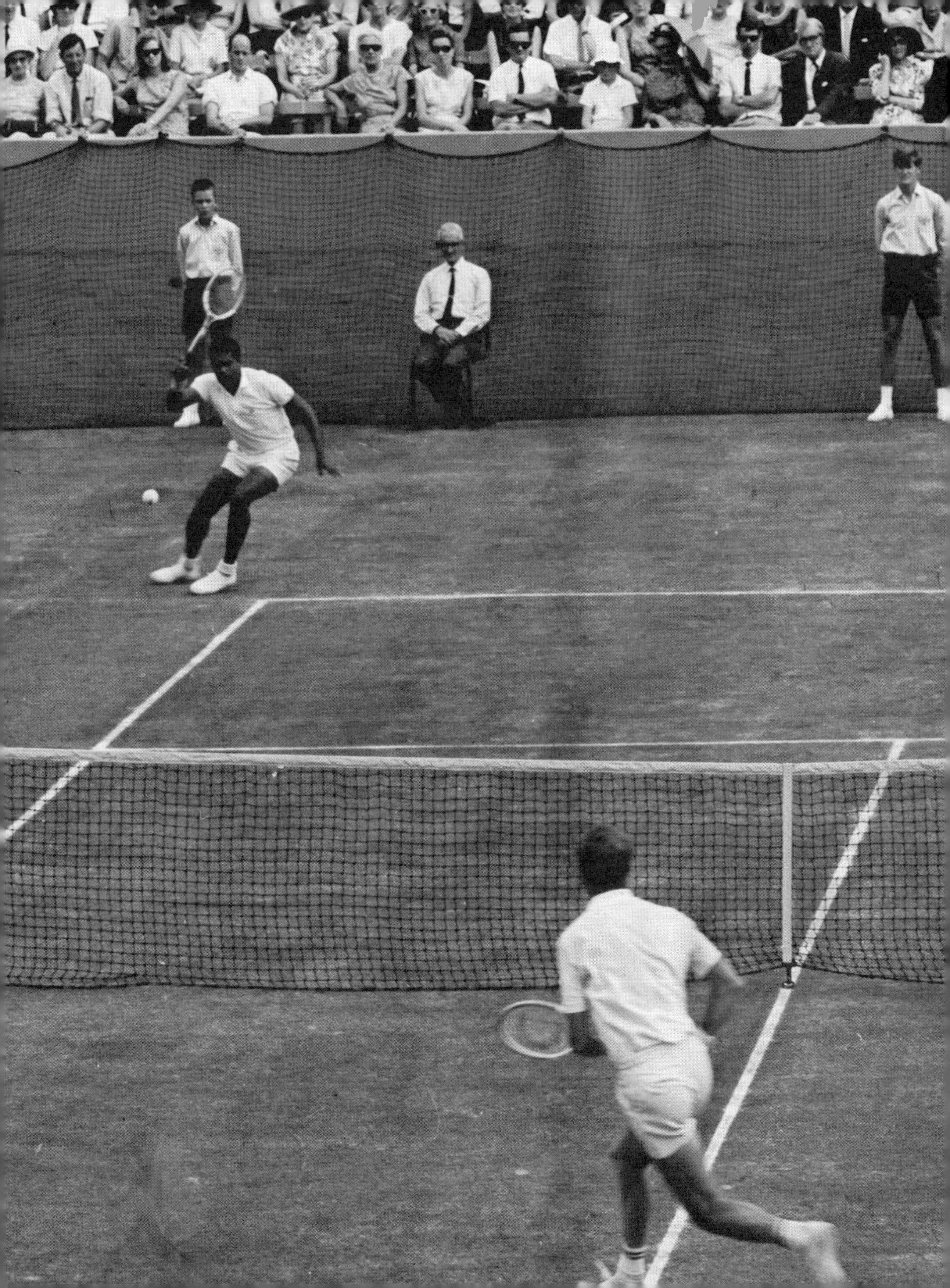

good workout; in ordinary doubles, the exchanges are seldom long enough or crisp enough even to work up a good sweat. Singles is also the choice of players who want to use, and be forced to use, all the strokes and shots. It is an all-court game, and when the ball comes to your weak backhand (to take an obvious example), there isn't a strong forehand there in the form of an aggressive partner to relieve the pressure.

A tactical challenge: Doubles is a game that demands close teamwork in order to execute an effective winning strategy.

Singles, in short, is the tennis version of bullfighting's *mano a mano.* It's just you and your opponent together on a court that can look awfully large when you're running down a drop shot and awfully small when you're trying to drive an approach shot into the backhand corner. If you relish head-to-head competion, with nobody to share the blame or credit for the outcome, singles is most assuredly your game.

A GAME OF COMPLEX STRATEGY

The matter of exercise aside, however, doubles satisfies a number of other basic sporting desires. If well played, it is a game of teamwork, a game in which one player's strength can and must complement that of his partner. At a high level, it is a game of complex strategy and tactics: parry alternates with thrust, soft shot with smash, low skimmer with high floater. The fundamental necessities are a consistently deep serve, a low service return, a strong first volley, an accurate overhead and a reliable lob. And the game is substantially enlivened by the unexpected gambit: the darting poach, the lob volley, the booming, down-the-line service return.

But doubles can be played quite successfully with a surprisingly limited array of shots, too. In fact, it can be played with not much more than fine athletic ability. Atlanta's Bobby Dodd, the longtime Georgia Tech football coach, had nothing resembling a normal tennis stroke; he pushed his serve into play and held the racquet in an awkward manner, often lobbing and volleying by holding it straight up or down with two hands on the grip. Yet Dodd, on a clay court, was a formidable doubles player. You had to be both clever and powerful to get a ball past him. There are Dodd-like characters, enjoying the competition and winning their share of matches, throughout the world of doubles.

Certain strokes, of course, take on a magnified importance in doubles: the overhead, volley, and lob, along with the serve and service return. Virtually any solid combination of these shots can make you at least a respectable doubles player and let the classic groundstrokers eat their hearts out.

Doubles offers another advantage in that few people play it really well. Few, that is, play it as the separate game it really is, rather than as an extension of singles. Thus, if you do concentrate on the game, you have a chance to stand out from the crowd, to put in their places all those players who play unthinking—and undistinguished—doubles.

THE FIVE KEYS TO SENIOR SUCCESS

Whether you prefer to play singles or doubles, you'll realize greater success and enjoyment by following these five fundamental principles:

1. Slow down and ease up. With very rare exceptions, senior tennis is not—and can't be—a power game. Don't attempt to charge the net on every point or blast your opponent off the court. Keep in mind Grand Master Ham Richardson's tongue-in-cheek comment on his ground game: "I used to use 10 calories to hit a forehand. Now I use only two."

2. Be steady and safe. Consistency will be your single greatest ally in any tennis match. Except for an occasional drop shot or wide-angle placement, hit balls that clear the net by a comfortable margin and land near the baseline. Play what Vic Seixas calls "the thinking man's game."

Seixas on consistency: Play "the thinking man's game."

3. Don't underestimate the age gap. Unless you're Frank Sedgman, six or seven years is the most you can give away to an opponent of equal ability and still expect to have a decent chance of winning.

4. Conserve energy. Catch your breath whenever you can without delaying play and avoid unnecessary effort. Pancho Gonzalez, before a big match, even refuses to sign autographs—an option to which we can all aspire.

5. Stay in shape. Conditioning determines the outcome of more senior matches than all the strokes combined. Settle on a suitable conditioning program and stick with it faithfully.

Shoring Up Your Strokes

At any age level, the sport of tennis constantly presents players with a number of challenges that beg to be met. And on the surface at least, it would seem that seniors, like yourself, face the tougher of those challenges. What's the saying, "You can't teach an old dog new tricks?"

If you're like a great many senior players, you probably talked yourself into believing that statement years ago. But it's just not true... especially in tennis.

In this chapter, we're going to look at one sure-fire way to put new zip in your game and then describe some of the important weapons you can and should have in your stroking arsenal.

ADD SPIN TO YOUR GAME

If there's one thing that a lot of senior players lack, it's variety in their shots. Take a good look at your ground strokes, for example. Chances are you hit the ball pretty flat. That stroking technique is great as far as making solid contact is concerned, but it has two big disadvantages: First, it gives your shots very little clearance over the net and second, it gives your opponent nice, predictable bounces just about every time.

How can you remedy the situation? By adding spin to your game—specifically topspin and underspin. Consider the advantages of each:

A topspin shot often clears the net by several feet—a very safe margin for error—and still stays in bounds. That makes it a high-percentage shot. But a ball hit with topspin also kicks high and toward the back fence when it bounces, giving your opponent a difficult, shoulder-high ball to return.

The underspin or "slice" shot, on the other hand, is relatively easy to control and requires far less energy to hit. When the ball bounces, it stays low to the court and forces an opponent to bend down to make a return, not a simple task for many older competitors.

Unfortunately, a lot of senior players who've become set in their ways believe it's exceptionally difficult to

How to hit with topspin: Swing from low to high with a firm wrist and finish with your racquet above head level (left). A topspin shot clears the net by several feet and kicks high when it bounces (see sketch of trajectory below).

hit balls with topspin or underspin. It's not. As a matter of fact, you probably use a little of both now on your "flat" ground strokes without even realizing it! That's because it's virtually impossible for you to hit a ball without imparting at least some degree of spin.

To hit a ground stroke with topspin, all you have to do is keep a firm wrist and swing forward from low to high, keeping your racquet face perpendicular to the ground throughout the stroke. This type of rising swing will cause you to contact the ball with an upward brushing motion. It's this brushing action that makes the ball rotate away from you as it travels across the net and that's what is called topspin. After you hit the ball, your racquet should continue on a rising path and finish well above the level of your head.

If you reverse your topspin stroking process and instead, swing from high to low so that you brush downward on the ball as you swing forward, you'll produce underspin. In other words, the ball will rotate back toward you as it flies over the net.

The next time you watch a pro match, notice that the players use spin on different shots to achieve specific goals. For example, most pros will hit slice shots when they approach the net to force their opponents to bend down low to make a return. Most of the time, such returns will be rising shots that can be volleyed easily at the net for winners. The underspin approach also travels relatively slowly through the air, so it allows the net rusher more time to move forward.

Topspin ground strokes are effective in another way. Their high, kicking bounces keep opponents pinned far behind their baselines. And when an opponent is

How to hit with underspin: Swing from high to low so that you brush downward on the ball as you swing forward (right). An underspin shot stays low to the court (see sketch of trajectory below), forcing an opponent to bend down to make a return.

camped at the net, a quickly dipping topspin shot often can force them to volley up to keep the ball in play. Such a topspin shot is especially effective in senior play because many older players can't bend well to hit that type of volley.

With some experimentation and practice hitting with spin, you can become a formidable senior player.

RE-THINK SHOT SELECTION PRIORITIES

As you get older, you have to do some rearranging of priorities as far as your shot selection goes. You have to shift away from relying on the strength of your serves and volleys to win points and instead, place more emphasis on other weapons, such as the lob and drop shot.

Here's a quick rundown on how you can best use the critical weapons in your stroking arsenal:

The Serve. Unless you're an unusual senior, you won't be blasting many service aces by your opponent in a match. As your age advances, the serve evolves to become more a means of putting the ball in play than a means of scoring points outright. Properly and intelligently hit, however, your serve can remain a potent weapon. It can force a weak return and open up the court for your next shot.

Your serve should be consistent, deep, and as unpredictable in pace and direction as you can make it. Consistency means being able to place six or seven out of every 10 first serves in play; less means you'll have to fall back too frequently on your second delivery, which is weaker and frequently may open the door to more double faults. Try to place your service deliveries well back in the service court, hopefully within a foot or so of the line; serves that bounce short of the center of the service court invite the receiver to take the offensive with forceful or sharply angled returns. And lastly, use a variety of serves to keep from becoming predictable. Remember, you always want to try to catch the receiver unaware to force a weak return.

Against most seniors, with their creaky knees and

Raw power: Pancho Gonzalez serves hard, even at middle age.

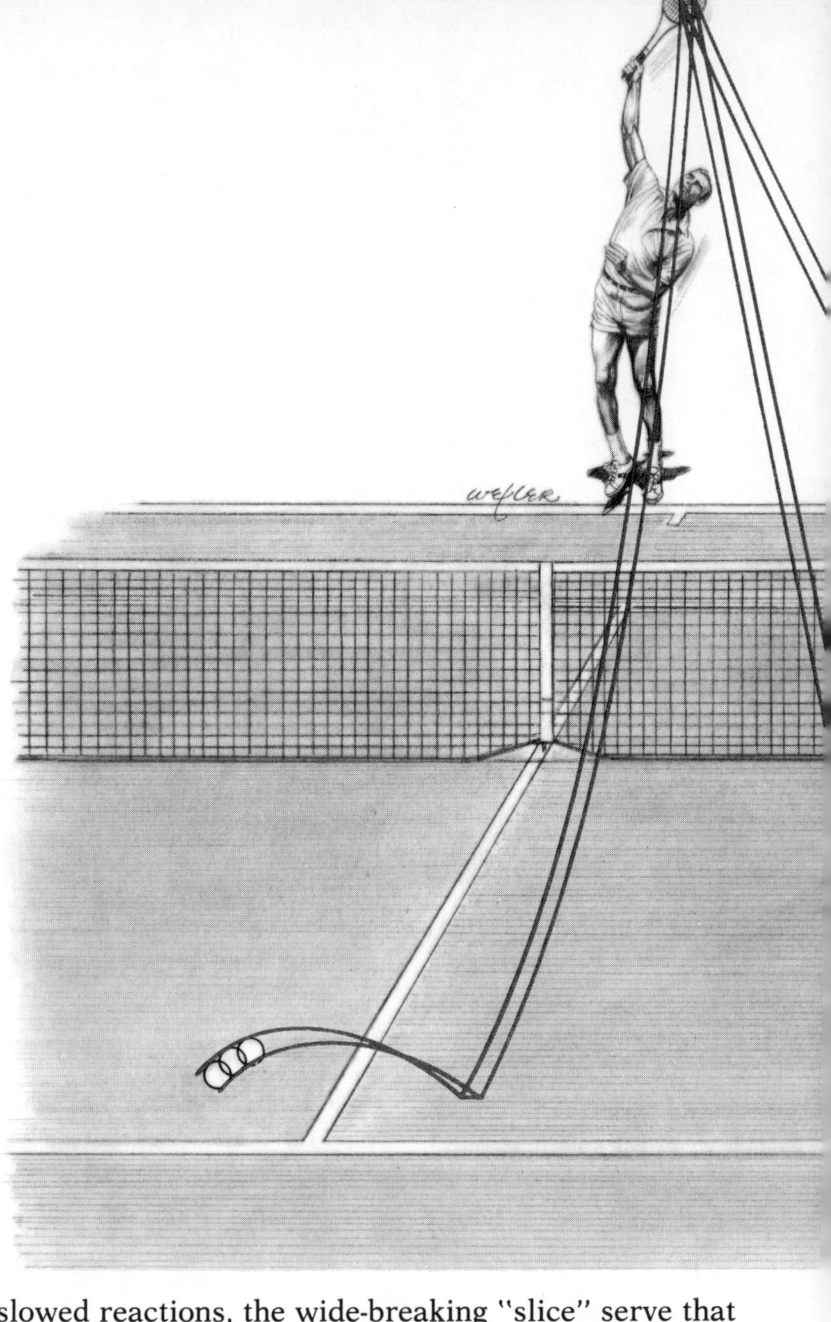

slowed reactions, the wide-breaking "slice" serve that bounces out beyond the doubles alley is most effective. For a right-hander, the slice serve works particularly well in serving to the forehand court because it spins away from the receiver and forces him out of position. On the backhand side, a good twist serve will accomplish the same purpose. A few wide serves, followed by well-placed shots to the opposite side of the court, will make your opponent wish you were hitting

Three effective serves: Don't be predictable with your deliveries. Use different types of spin and placement to keep opponents honest.

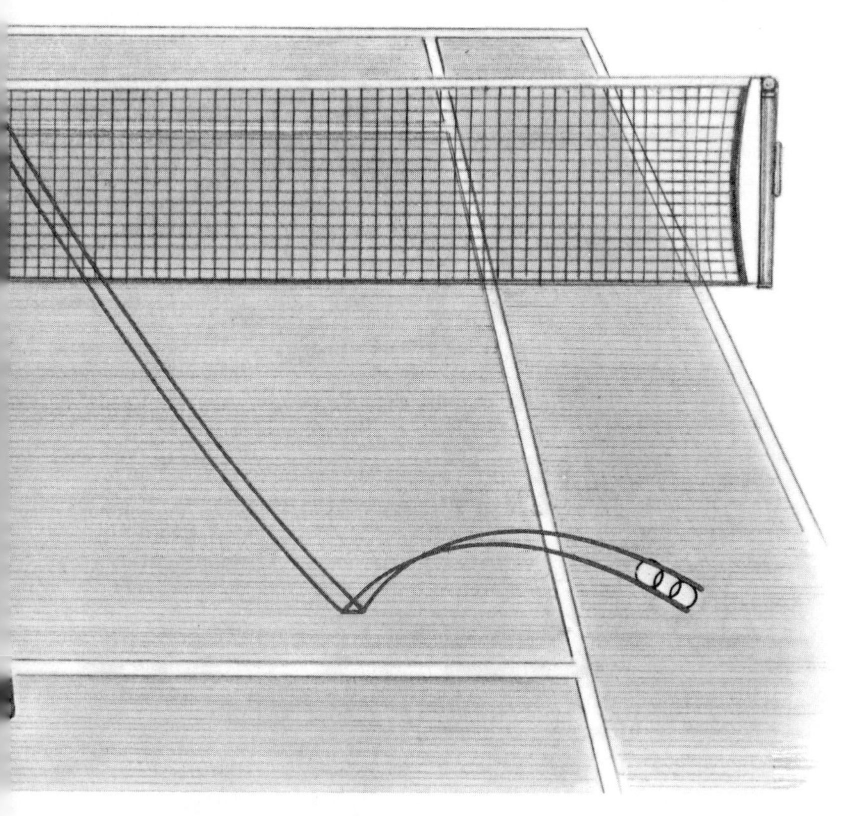

flat, hard serves instead.

If you do have a hard serve, don't abandon it completely. Mix it in with the rest of your deliveries. Use it when you can afford to gamble—say, when you enjoy a 40-love lead or when you spot the receiver moving forward in anticipation of a soft serve. When you do serve hard, try hitting directly at the receiver. Because they're not so agile, older players have a difficult time handling hard deliveries to the navel.

The Lob. In good senior doubles matches at almost any level, you're likely to see the air filled with lobs. And logically so, from the standpoint of the player hitting one. The lob is the safest of all shots in that it affords the widest tolerance for error over the net and is very difficult to return for a winner—provided the ball is hit deep enough. It can also be very effective in terms of tiring an opponent and forcing either a mis-hit or a weak return through frustration.

Most seniors have neither the power nor the coordination to hit a series of strong, effective overhead smashes. It takes legs with a lot of resiliency and spring to constantly run down deep lobs and help provide the power to crack overhead winners.

Beginning players think of the lob as the shot you hit when you're so extended or out of position you can't hit anything else. Certainly, it has that basic defensive function. But the lob becomes a valuable tool, too, in the following ways: as a maneuver that changes the pace of a rally and buys you time so you can catch your breath; that gives aggressive, perhaps overanxious, opponents the opportunity to make an error; that exploits a weak overhead; and that has the potential to win a point outright.

These cases, of course, refer to the *offensive* lob, a highly effective, but often underused, weapon in senior tennis. With it, you can catch an opponent at the net by surprise. Chances are he'll be leaning forward, waiting to jump on your passing shot attempt as you loop the ball over his head.

Depth and height are the prime ingredients in any good lob. It you hit one defensively, be sure to place the ball as deep in the court as you safely can. Use plenty of height because you're buying time to scramble back into position. Also, lots of players have difficulty handling a high-hit ball dropping nearly straight down at them. The offensive lob, on the other hand, should be hit with a lower trajectory so that the net rusher won't be able to scramble back and recover it. Depth is im-

Time to recover: Sven Davidson (right) hits a defensive lob to catch his breath.

Lobbing tactics: When you're out of position, send up a high defensive lob. If you're inside the baseline, try the offensive shot.

portant, but surprise and placement are the major keys to the shot. Use topspin if you can. It will carry the ball quickly over your opponent's head and make it bounce away from him, toward the back fence.

As far as direction is concerned, unless your opponent has a very weak overhead, the lob most often should be directed over his backhand side. The backhand overhead is an extremely difficult shot, and even those who hit it consistently can seldom generate much power.

What's that? You say you don't have control of your lobs? You may be taking too large a backswing and slapping at the ball. Cut your normal ground-stroke backswing in half and stroke through the ball fully, using a complete follow-through. Your control of the shot should improve markedly.

The Overhead. If your opponents are smart, they'll give you your fill of lobs. But don't be discouraged; well-played overheads, even if they don't put holes in the back fence, usually can overcome the most persistent lobbers.

To hit an effective overhead, you first must concentrate on getting into the right position and keeping your eye on the ball as you hit it. What's the "right" posi-

Heads-up overhead: Ulrich keeps his eyes on the ball.

tion? Pancho Gonzalez has a graphic way of describing it: "The point where the ball would hit you between the eyes if it continued to fall." Neale Fraser, who still hits a crushing overhead, adds two other tips: "Always turn sideways to the net, and point your forward shoulder at the ball as it descends."

Tactically, you shouldn't try to "kill" or put away an overhead unless you're close to the net. Try for angles and, if you're forced back behind the service line, drive the ball deep and look for a shorter return. Good depth and use of court angles on the overhead are especially

Lob antidote: Angle off your overheads for winners.

important in doubles, where lobs fly frequently and the opposition, playing deep in the backcourt, can send back hard smashes hit directly at them. Don't hesitate to let a lob, especially a high, deep one bounce: Hitting on the bounce requires less-precise timing than connecting with the ball as it descends. One time *not* to let the ball bounce is when your opponent is clearly out of position and his lob is shallow. You don't want to give him the opportunity to scramble back.

As for the topspin lob, it is, as we mentioned earlier, a difficult shot to control. Realistically, it can't be learned apart from other topspin strokes. In other words, if you don't have a topspin backhand drive, you're not going to be able to develop a topspin backhand lob. If the stroke intrigues you, try to take a stab at learning it. If you fail, the ordinary lob, properly executed, will do very nicely.

The Drop Shot. While a good drop shot is effective in any age group, it is a standard ploy in the senior game. When it's used wisely, nothing can so predictably tire and exasperate your opponent.

The drop shot can be hit in two ways: by "bunting" the ball low over the net, or by undercutting it to produce a backspin shot that loops over the net. In either case, the ball must land closer to the net than to the service line to be effective. Accomplished players prefer using the backspin shot, and for good reason—backspin makes the ball bounce low and straight up or, in the case of extreme spin, back toward the net, so that the

Senior ploy: Anderson uses the drop shot to tire an opponent.

shot is more difficult to retrieve.

In senior play, the drop shot has three valuable functions: to win points outright, to set up a weak return that enables you to take charge of the point and to wear down your opponent. Those are hefty dividends from just one shot.

But beware the potential pitfalls of the drop shot. It's a low-percentage stroke. Unless you possess incredible touch, don't try to hit one from more than a few steps behind the service line; otherwise, you'll make too many errors and give your opponent too much time to "read" the shot. Also, rarely resort to it on match or set point; that's simply too risky. Finally, don't overplay the shot and use it so often that your opponent can anticipate it.

The last point needs elaboration. Against a quality player, any good shot can be repeated too often, allowing him to anticipate, prepare and compensate, all to your ultimate detriment. He who lives by the drop shot can die by it, too. Whitney Reed is a living testament to that rule. Reed, whose game is based on touch, has a first-class drop shot. But even he admits that he tends to go to it too often.

More than any other stroke, the drop shot's effectiveness is enhanced by disguise. Don't use footwork and a backswing that telegraph your intentions. Learn to hit the shot with the same footwork and backswing that you use for a regular ground stroke and you'll almost certainly catch your opponent off balance.

When should you try hitting a drop shot? Well, you can improve your chances of successfully using the shot by waiting until you can see that your opponent is tired. That way, he probably won't have the speed or strength left to reach the ball. Don Budge has a divergent theory, though: Drop shot *early* when an opponent is a little stiff and uncoordinated. Some players, Budge reasons, get faster as the match goes on. In middle age, however, not many of your opponents are likely to get faster in the late stages of a match. Let the match situation be your guide on court. Study your opponent and his reaction to your shots and play accordingly.

The deadly drop shot: Hit properly, it can wear down an opponent (right), win a point outright, or force a weak return.

Delicate touch: Drop volleys require a relaxed arm and slightly laid-back racquet head (above), as Anderson shows on the facing page.

The Drop Volley. This close relative of the drop shot is a delicate and risky maneuver. If the drop shot requires a lot of touch, the drop volley—caressing a hard-hit ball barely over the net, rather than punching it deep into the court—requires even more. Only advanced players need apply.

Reed is also a past master of the drop volley—from as far back as the service line. So is one of the past decade's outstanding seniors, Gus Palafox. At his best, Palafox combined pace with finesse, a forceful volleying game with a deft drop volley.

Basically, however, the drop volley is a loser's shot. On critical points, many more players, including professionals, will miss the shot than will make it. So ration your drop volleys accordingly.

Half volley key: A shoulder turn (above) is all that's needed to take your racquet back for the shot. Sedgman shows you how on the next page.

The Half Volley. A standard shot for anyone who wants to take the net, the half volley becomes more important as you slow down with age. Why? Because you won't be able to reach the forecourt as quickly as you once did, more balls will land at your feet. You won't have any choice but to get down low to the ball and hit a half volley.

Wherever you're positioned, don't forget that the half volley is a defensive type of shot. It requires too much touch and timing to be hit aggressively. So you should learn to control the direction and depth of the shot, according to your opponent's position. When he is in the backcourt, play the half volley deep or, if you're feeling lucky, short enough to win the point outright. When

he's at net, as in a doubles volleying exchange, play the shot low and at his feet, hoping that his own half volley will float up and enable you to hit down for a winner.

Remember that the half volley is a genuine stroke, not merely a block. You should take a very short backswing and meet the ball well in front of you, using a gentle, but firm, scooping motion. The keys to the shot are bending the knees and hitting the ball just after it bounces, like a baseball infielder playing a ground ball on the short hop.

Changing Pace for Singles Success

The aging process shows no favorites. Sooner or later, depending on our fitness regimens, all of us lose a step or two of quickness, a little bit of power and the ability to put away shots as authoritatively as we once did.

Some senior players try to ignore this trend and continue to use the same tactics they won with in their youth. Usually, they lose their matches. Smart seniors, however, alter their playing strategy to fit their physical condition and win.

THE WINNING BASICS

What is a sound, basic singles strategy for middle-aged players? Bobby Riggs, as usual, gets right to the heart of the matter: "Do you know anybody who likes balls hit softly at 'em? Make the other guy generate his own pace."

Riggs has practiced that strategy throughout his tennis career. You have to be very talented, as he was, to make it work against strong, young opponents, but you can be just average in ability and succeed with it in the senior game. Why? Because successfully combatting a soft hitter, someone who hits a lot of "junk" shots, requires the utmost in patience, an overall soundness of strokes and the ability to consistently produce forcing shots. Few middle-aged players possess this rare combination of qualities.

But hitting without pace is only one part of a basic, winning singles strategy. Depth, a great equalizer in senior tennis, is the other. It puts the smooth, sound strokers and the awkward retrievers on the same level. If you keep your opponent pinned behind the baseline, except when you use occasional drop shots and wide angles, he'll have a tough time beating you. After all, he can't charge the net from deep in his own court.

From these two general tactics, you can see that the bottom line in senior tennis is to keep the ball in play. Don't go for many winners or try to hit too close to the lines. And when you have a chance to generate some offense, don't attempt to win the point immediately

Riggs on singles: "Do you know anybody who likes balls hit softly at 'em? Make the other guy generate his own pace."

with your first shot. Use it to force a weak return that will give you the clear upper hand. Then, let your second or third shot provide the payoff.

At this juncture, you may be wondering what you'll look like on the court hitting soft floaters, merely staying in the point and waiting for the occasional error or opportunity to attack to surface. If so, you need to learn a fundamental lesson of senior tennis: Forget about "looking good." If you want to win as a senior, you'll have to throw away your pretensions—whatever memories or dreams you harbor about playing in an aggressive, hard-running, hard-hitting style. Sure, you'll still have opportunities to hit decisively and to knock off an overhead or volley. But basically, your game will be built on consistency, good shot placement and patience.

You might find encouragement, and consolation if you need it, in the playing adjustment that Neale Fraser has made now that he's a senior. As a young man, Fraser was one of the most relentlessly aggressive players the sport has known. Had he tried to remain so as a senior, he could not have succeeded as a Grand Master. He had to adapt, and he did.

As Fraser puts it, "Now that I have a little bit older head on my shoulders"—and, he could add, a less springy pair of legs under him—"I realize that it's not necessary to hit a lot of winners or a lot of balls so close to the line or the top of the net. You can force errors instead."

How do you force those errors and produce offensive opportunities? By changing your overall strategy of steady baseline play just enough to keep your opponents off balance . . . and out of breath.

TACTICAL VARIATIONS

When you want to "win" a point, rather than wait for your opponent to lose one, you have a number of options. Here are four of the most effective:

1. Hit wide rather than deep. Bill Talbert, a tennis great who directs the U.S. Open, observes that today's younger players do not exploit the full width of the court. He's quite right, but maybe it's not necessary for

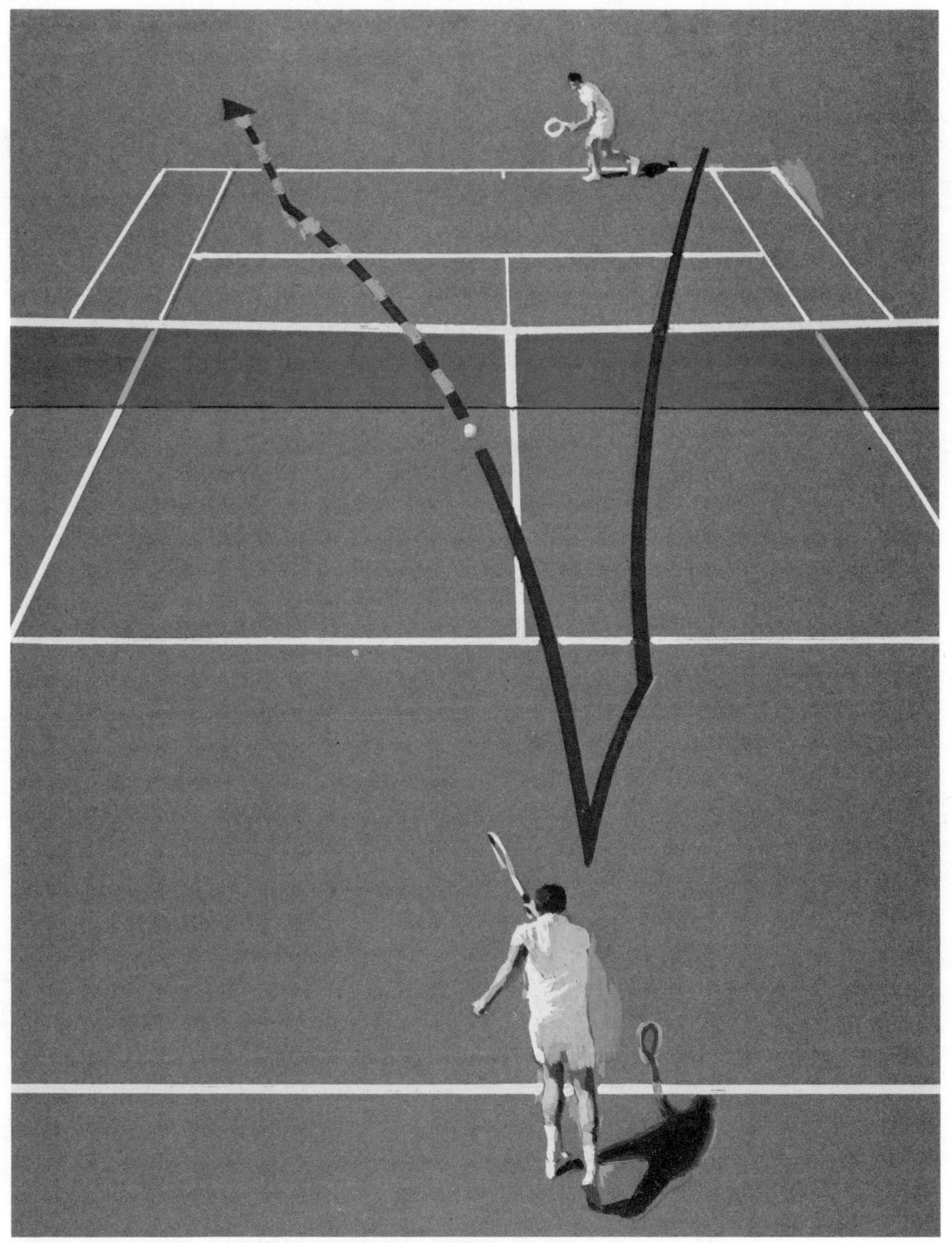

Wear down opponents: Solid ground strokes to the corners will exploit the full width of the tennis court.

the young guys who are armed with so much raw power. For seniors trying to take the offensive, though, it's virtually mandatory.

Just think about the difference for a second. The young player, drawn short and wide, often will reach the ball easily, probably chip it down the line, and move in toward the net to volley. However, the senior will get there with difficulty and, in most cases, be unable to go on the offensive. He'll probably try to hit the ball back high and deep to gain time to recover his court position. The only problem is he can't recover quickly enough. If he hits anything less than a good shot, his opponent is in control, with at least half an open court to hit into.

Solid ground strokes to the corners are the standard weapons you can use to exploit the full width of the court and tire an opponent. The angled drop shot can be effective, too, if you have a lot of touch. Two world-class seniors, Pancho Segura and Sweden's Torsten Johannsen, have made the shot something of an art form.

2. Go to the net occasionally. Assuming you're a capable volleyer, don't abandon net play entirely. You need to advance to your forecourt once in a while to take advantage of a short, weak shot and assume an offensive position. By moving in to the net, you'll intimidate a lot of senior players who feel more comfortable in a baseline-to-baseline stroking rally.

Generally, a good time to take the net is when you're playing on a fast court surface. Many of the all-weather surfaces, as well as grass, produce a quick, low bounce that adds some punch to an ordinary serve and helps make standard volleys winners.

"Most of volleying," Frank Sedgman says, "is being in the right position early enough." That means you should always try to cut off your opponent's angles of return when you're at the net. How? By moving a little further toward the alley when your approach shot takes your opponent wide. This positioning will force him to hit a perfect shot to get the ball past you.

When you do take the net, whatever the court

Attack short balls: Deep approach shots will allow you to advance to the forecourt and take command of play.

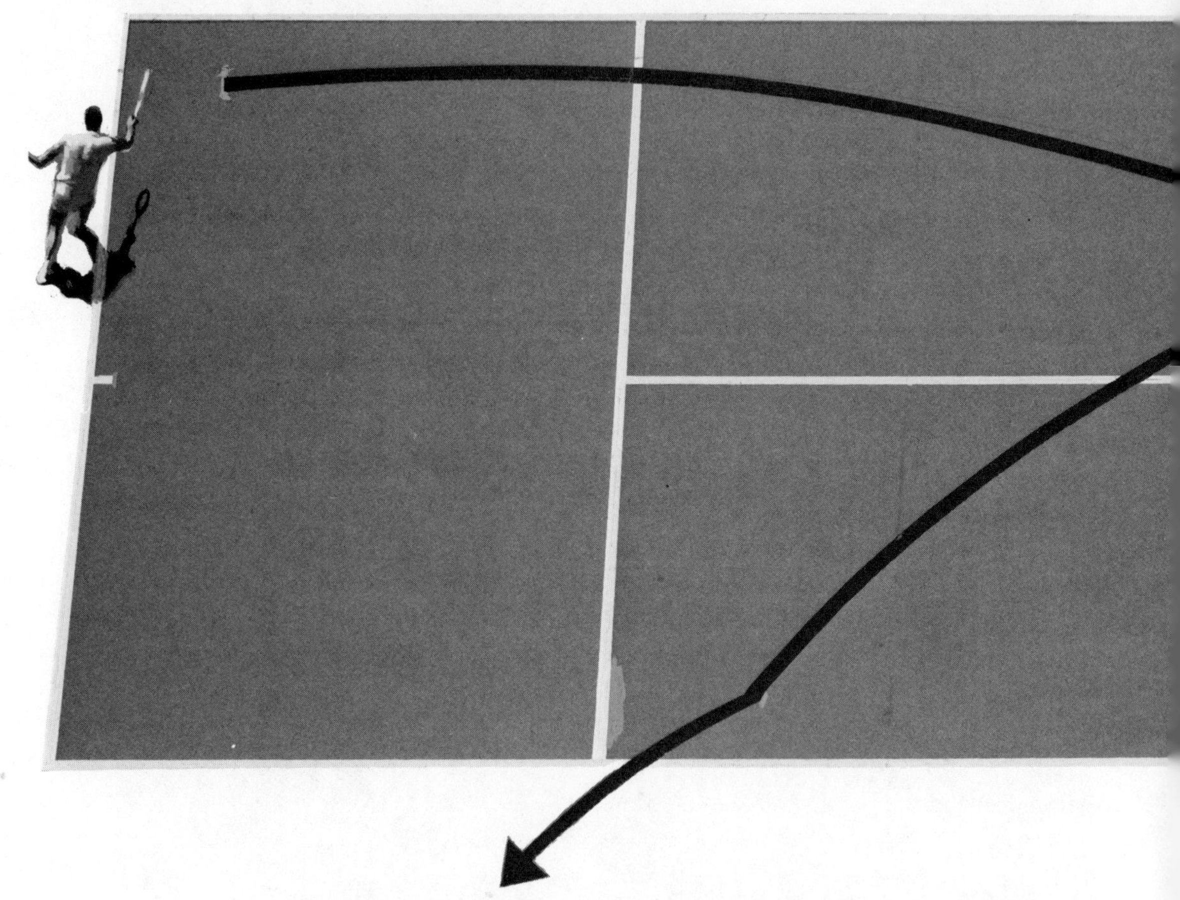

surface, go for a winning volley. The forecourt is no place from which to keep the ball in play. If you do, you'll probably lose the point to a good lob or passing shot. When you do get a lob, don't try to power the overhead through your opponent unless he's fairly close to the net. Angle your overhead to make him run and to open up the court for your next shot. Remember that your volley is only as good as your overhead. In the senior game, that maxim holds especially true.

3. Serve with a purpose in mind. Although your serve may not be the powerful weapon it once was, it can be a lot more than simply a means of putting the ball into

play. Serving wide, of course, pulls your opponent off the court and any tactic that accomplishes that task creates offensive opportunities for you. Serving straight at him can also produce a weak return. If you can get some power behind it, the straight-on serve exploits the typical senior's slowed reflexes and lessened agility; a hard serve to the navel may well set you up with an easy mid-court shot.

Put-away points: Once you get into good volleying position, you should be able to put away any rising shots quickly.

And if you're hitting good serves, don't be afraid to follow them occasionally to the net. You may get a "sitter" to volley away, and, in any event, you'll start your opponent second-guessing your intentions. That's often worth several points a match.

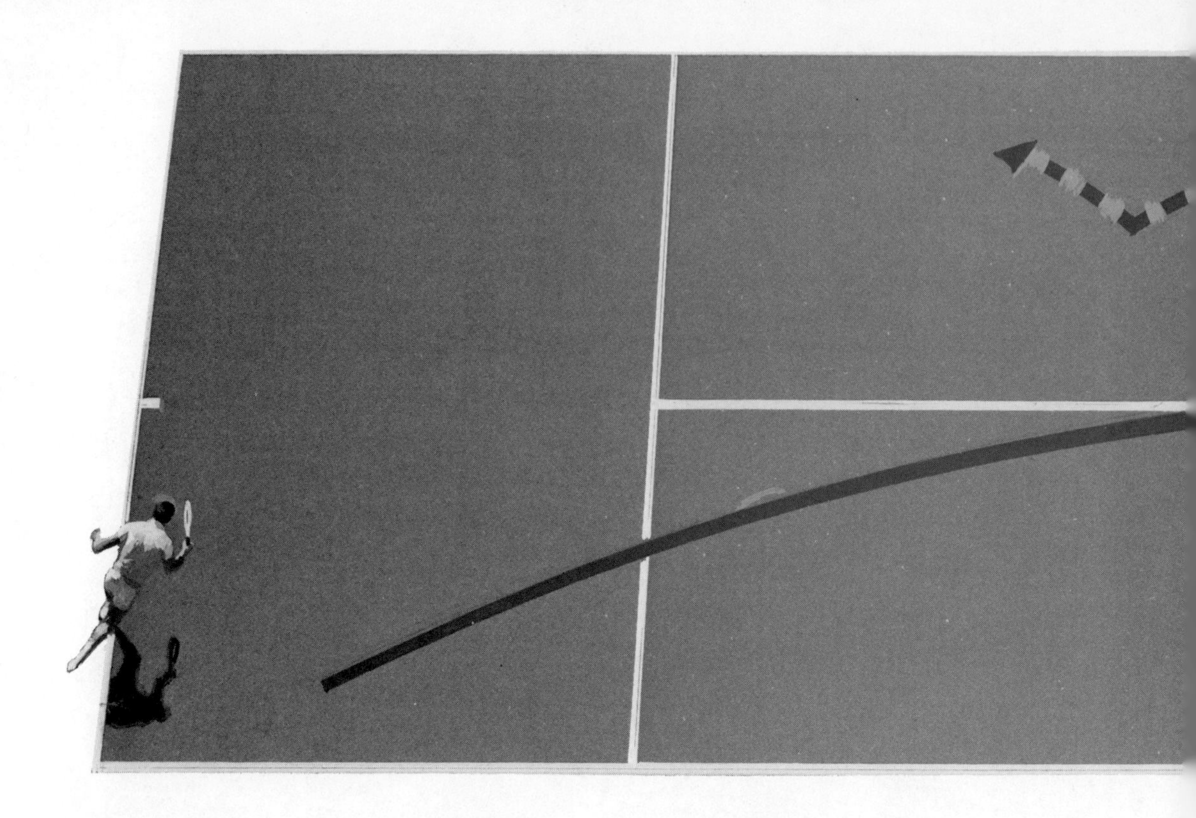

4. Use the drop shot-lob combination. This is the one-two punch of senior tennis and if it doesn't do the job the first time in a point, you can often repeat it for the knockout. The effective shot combination also helps you get a leg up on the next two or three points, as your opponent struggles to catch his breath.

HOW TO DIG YOURSELF OUT OF A HOLE

O.K., let's say you're playing from the baseline, hitting soft and deep, waiting for errors, trying an occasional offensive foray. But so is your opponent, and he's winning. What do you do?

One of the oldest axioms in tennis advises: "Always change a losing game." That sounds logical, and it is, *if* you have other tactics to switch to. If, for example, you're a senior baseliner who can still volley crisply and put away an overhead, don't stay at the baseline when you're being beaten there. Instead, take the net and hope that your opponent's passing shots and lobs are less effective than his deep ground strokes. You can

also make greater use of the tactical variations outlined earlier. Use more wide angles, drop shots and hard serves. Try some "moonballs," or lob-like ground strokes; most players hate to deal with those. Hit some slices and chops. Do anything—anything ethical—to disrupt your opponent's rhythm and get him out of his groove. Remember, you have nothing to lose and you might still be able to turn the match around.

However, if you're a one-style player, changing tactics will probably only hasten your defeat. Your only real option in this case is to work twice as hard at winning with your single style. Primarily, that means concentrating better on every shot. For both forehands and backhands, get your racquet back early, consciously shift your weight forward into the ball, and make your shot clear the net by plenty. If you've been hitting late or in a jerky fashion, this back-to-basics approach should get your strokes back into gear.

Also, beware of falling into two common traps: One is failing to watch the ball closely, and the other is getting the racquet back too late.

Change a losing game: When you get a short ball, try hitting a short ball yourself to force your opponent to come to the net. He may feel uneasy there.

Both errors are difficult to correct and you're not likely to approach perfection on either of them. But you can make a marked improvement by following a couple of practical suggestions.

First, to minimize your eye-off-the-ball problem, you should think to yourself, "I'm going to watch the racquet hit the ball—the moment of impact." You can't, of course, because the ball is on your strings only a scant fraction of a second. But the attempt will help you focus your concentration on the ball. As a result, you should make fewer mis-hits because you'll have better timing.

The answer to late preparation is to start your backswing as soon as you know which way your opponent's shot is headed, either to your forehand or backhand side. That will overcome the tendency to delay taking your racquet back until the ball has crossed the net—or even until it has bounced in front of you. And if you have to run wide to retrieve a shot, don't wait until you get into position to begin your backswing. Get your racquet back *as* you run, so you're ready to make the forward swing as soon as you reach the ball.

Middle-aged players routinely make several other playing errors that prevent them from winning more matches:

1. Attempting to make too good a shot. Riggs calls this "trying to play better than you know how," which, he says, "works once in a million times." Well, the odds probably are a bit better than that, but they're never favorable—for every difficult winner you pull off, you'll hit many more tough losers. You should make a realistic assessment of your shotmaking abilities and play within them. Stick with the high-percentage shots.

2. Hitting too close to the top of the net. Tennis, especially senior tennis, is a game won by opponents' errors. And a large percentage of those errors come from failing to clear the net by a comfortable margin on ground strokes. The net-skimmer runs the risk not only of losing the point outright by netting the ball, but of setting up his opponent for an easy approach shot,

Poised to swing: Anderson brings his racquet back early.

should his shot barely clear the net and fall short in the opposite court. You should hit low only when your opponent is *at* the net, or when you're trying a short angled shot to pull him out of position. At other times, keep the ball several feet above the net. That will give your shots safe clearance over the net and ensure good depth as well.

3. Using poor footwork. Weak shots will often result if you don't get your feet (and therefore your body) into the proper position for the stroke you have to execute. This mistake is most obvious and damaging on ground strokes, where the foot opposite your racquet hand should be pointed toward the net when you're in hitting position, ready to receive the weight coming forward as you make your swing. "Most people get to the ball on the wrong foot, with an open stance," says Alex Olmedo, a former Grand Master who's had many years of teaching experience. As a solution, Olmedo recommends dancing—"something that imitates the little two-step you do on the court to get into proper hitting position."

4. Missing too many first serves. You should always strive to make your first serve a model of consistency, placement, and depth. In senior tennis, all three rate higher priorities than power. If need be, take some speed *off* your first serve to make sure it goes in close to 70 percent of the time.

5. Playing on an infrequent basis. Getting out on court to hit only 20 minutes a day is much better than playing for an hour-and-a-half once a week. That's true for conditioning as well as for strokes. A daily workout, even against a backboard or garage door, will keep you limber and maintain the eye-hand coordination essential for competitive tennis. According to Grand Master Sven Davidson, it will also ward off tennis elbow. That malady, Davidson says, tends to arrive when you start hitting a lot of balls after a long, inactive layoff.

Winning With Opportunistic Doubles

Unfortunately, almost all beginners and many intermediates treat doubles as an extension of singles play. Since middle-aged players tend to devote larger portions of their court time to doubles, understanding the differences between the two games and playing accordingly is particularly important.

Doubles is practically a game unto itself. It calls for strategies, tactics, strokes, and a few maneuvers—such as poaching—that are never seen on the singles court. When properly played, doubles is an exercise in angles

and net-skimming returns interspersed with timely lobs. As Bill Talbert, a longtime doubles champion, has written: "There is no game like it for the continuous pressure of tactical concentration, plus split-second timing."

Talbert adds that it is the game for the middle-age years, when tennis players "wake up to the fact that doubles is really a better game than singles or any other sport you may care to mention." While that may be the doubles champion's bias showing, there is no doubt that doubles is a marvelous game and that it can assume even more competitive dimensions as a player learns its subtle nuances and demands.

An exercise in angles: Doubles assumes even more competitive dimensions as you learn its subtle nuances and demands.

OFFENSIVE TACTICS

A Riggs-like singles strategy of hitting deep without much pace won't work in doubles matches. That's because an opposing net player can easily pick off those shots. So in doubles matches, you and your partner want to be the first ones to take control of the net during a point and thereby gain a substantial offensive edge. From the forecourt, your team can apply a great deal of pressure on opponents to hit great passing shots, deep lobs or accurate "dink" shots at your feet.

Net play in senior doubles, however, calls for a certain amount of patience and maneuvering; you often cannot put the ball away on the very first shot. Instead, you have to create the opportunity for a putaway. Frank Sedgman talks about playing "defensive doubles" as a senior, but that term seems a little too passive. "Opportunistic doubles" would be a more accurate description for senior play. The challenge of the game is to keep as much pressure on the opponents as you safely can, and wait for the first good chance to end the point.

The same playing philosophy applies when both teams are at the net, which to many devotees is the quintessential doubles moment. Your objective in this situation is to keep volleys low to force opponents to hit a rising shot that you can pounce on—in a phrase, hitting down so they'll hit up.

As in senior singles play, it's important to use the entire width of the court in doubles by hitting more angled shots. With two players covering the court on each side of the net, it's hard to find openings and that task becomes harder if you keep putting the ball between the singles sidelines. The angled shot, drawing one of the opponents into or beyond the doubles alleys, is one of the most reliable ways to create those openings.

THE IMPORTANCE OF TEAMWORK

Having a partner on your side of the net reduces the amount of territory you have to cover in a match but also adds the responsibility or need for teamwork and communication. In a close match, these two doubles essentials play decisive roles. Teamwork in doubles starts even before the first point is played in a match.

Working together: Ulrich (right) talks with his partner, Sedgman, about strategy. Communication is vital in doubles.

Some discussion is helpful to answer the following questions:

1. Which side of the court should you play? Most teams answer this question by automatically positioning the player with the better backhand in the "ad" or left court. However, there are other important factors to consider. For example, who has the better overhead? If both players are right-handed, the one in the "ad" court will be in the natural overhead position to cover lobs hit down the center. Another consideration is, who is the stronger player? Usually, the better player should take the "ad" court because he'll have to face the critical points (ad-in and ad-out) during the other team's service games. However, there is another point of view that suggests the stronger player take the deuce court because he can put you into game-point situations.

Quick decisions: When a ball is hit down the middle, the player with the more reliable shot required should play the ball.

2. Who should handle shots down the middle? Ground strokes or lobs hit down the center can create confusion between partners because oftentimes, they'll both be able to reach the ball. As a general rule, though, the nod should go to the player who has the stronger, more reliable stroke that's required. In other words, if your opponents send up a lob down the middle and you have a better overhead than your partner, you should make the shot.

3. Should the netman poach? Poaching, an aggressive move in which the netman, after his partner serves, leaves his half of the court to intercept the service return, can pay big dividends in a senior doubles match. Even if an attempt is unsuccessful, it can instill an element of doubt in the receiver's mind and force a weak return or two on subsequent points.

In the final analysis, the success of the ploy depends on several factors: the netman's quickness and timing, his volleying ability, the strength of his partner's serve and the accuracy of the receiver's return. From a team standpoint, the important thing is that each player know how disposed his partner is to poaching and in what sorts of situations (for instance, at ad-in on a serve down the center line). Experienced teams sometimes use hand signals (behind the netman's back) to announce a poach before the serve. These signals can be very simple: a closed fist indicates a poaching attempt, for example. Of course, a casual word, *sotto voce,* between points also will convey the message adequately.

Other matters also need to be settled in a pre-match discussion. Will the receiver's partner stand in the forecourt or at the baseline? If the partner is playing "up," will the receiver follow his service return to the net? For that matter, will both servers routinely follow their own serves to the net?

Once play begins, another element of teamwork is essential—moving together during a point to allow maximum court coverage. Examples include running back to retrieve a lob hit over your partner's head, switching to the other side of the court when he's retrieving one over *your* head, and moving toward the center when your partner has to cover a shot down the alley. Movement by both partners is imperative. "If the ball is hit to the left," Pancho Gonzalez has written, "your team should move to the left almost as though the two of you were connected by a 12-foot rope."

An aggressive move: Poaching (right) can instill an element of doubt in the receiver's mind and force a weak return or two on subsequent points.

EXPLOIT YOUR SERVING ADVANTAGE

The serving team owns a bigger advantage in doubles than a lone player does in singles. To maximize the advantage, you should adhere to the following time-tested tactical principles:

Serve under control and with depth. The power serve plays a minor role in doubles. When it goes in, the hard serve affords little time for the server to reach the forecourt and can be returned easily with a lob or a simple "block" shot. And when it misses, it can set the stage for a second serve that the receiver can attack and return forcefully.

So save the hard, cannonball serve for an occasional change of pace. Hit your first serve at three-quarter-speed with spin for control. Above all, place it deep and into one of the corners of the service box. Depth, direction, and consistency (about 70 percent of first deliveries in play) are the hallmarks of an effective doubles serve. If yours has all three, you'll have time to move into fine volleying position.

Rex Hartwig, the former Grand Master, has long been living proof of the power of a consistent first serve. In doubles, he seldom serves at more than half-speed. Yet in winning the U.S. doubles title in 1953, he held service 37 straight times. Hartwig moves the serve around like a great control pitcher in baseball works the strike zone. His arching, slow-moving ball lands so deep that even his short legs can carry him a step or two inside the service line—just the right position for volleying away a poor return.

Bill Talbert's fine book, "The Game of Doubles in Tennis," gives striking confirmation of the first-serve rule. Talbert notes that in a professional match in the early 1950s pitting Sedgman and Ken McGregor against

The serving edge: Save your hard, cannonball delivery for an occasional change of pace. Hit your first serve at three-quarter speed with spin for control (right).

Jack Kramer and Pancho Segura, the servers won 82 percent of the points when the first serve was good and a mere 24 percent when they had to fall back on the second delivery.

Poach now and then. A good ground-stroker likes nothing better in doubles than to groove his service return low and at the feet of the server, if he's coming to net. One of the best ways to break that pattern is for the server's partner to poach to intercept some of those good returns.

Poaching requires precise timing, though. And the key to a successful poach is to move as soon as the receiver has committed himself to hit in a certain direction. Usually, that point occurs a split second before he's about to make contact with the ball. If you move too soon, an alert receiver will place his shot behind you and out of the reach of your partner. Of course, learning to correctly anticipate the receiver's point of commitment isn't easy; practice and experience are important.

As mentioned earlier in this chapter, you should communicate your poaching intentions to the server. But whether or not he's had advance warning, the server should move quickly to cover the half of the court the poacher vacates.

Throw in an odd serving formation. Are you losing too many points to crosscourt service returns? Try the reverse service positioning, often called the Australian formation (it's said to have been invented Down Under). Server and netman stand on the same side of the center line in this serving configuration. The simple switch virtually obliges the receiver to return down the line instead of crosscourt—a tougher, low-percentage shot.

The Australian formation can also be used to take the

A challenging alignment: The Australian serving formation (right) forces the receiver to hit a more difficult down-the-line return.

pressure off a weak backhand volley. If you volley poorly on that side, for instance, serving Australian-style to the "ad" court will bring almost every return to your forehand side.

When serving to the deuce court in this formation, however, aim for the receiver's backhand to minimize the danger of a strong forehand return down the alley or angled sharply crosscourt. And don't overwork the formation or the opposition may figure out how to counteract it.

Stay back on serve if it suits you. Common doubles strategy dictates that the server follow his delivery to the net. That wisdom is supposed to hold even for seniors, who may be slow getting to the service line or may lack good volleying reflexes or overheads.

Certainly, the classic tennis strategy offers big tactical advantages. But how much of an advantage do you enjoy if you can't execute the shots—volleys and overheads—on which the advantage depends? Although it offends doubles purists, there's nothing at all wrong with the server remaining at the baseline. That way, at least, if your ground strokes and lobs are far better than your net game, you'll stand a better chance of holding serve.

Generally, though, it's not wise for the server to remain at the baseline if his partner is stationed at net. If you do, you'll leave open a huge diagonal area of court between you, which decent volleyers on the other side can easily exploit.

BLUNT THE SERVER'S EDGE

If you and your partner are both able to hold serve throughout a match, all you need is one service break a set to notch a victory. Here's how you can set up those breaks:

Neutralizing a serve: Probably the best service return in doubles is one that's hit low at the server's feet (right). He won't be able to volley the ball offensively.

Return serve low. A low service return seldom can be volleyed for a winner and will force the server, if he's coming to net, to hit up on the ball to clear the net. His shot may float high enough to allow you or your partner to close in on the net and put it away. "Get it at the guy's feet when he comes in," Hartwig says. "That's what returning serve in doubles is all about."

In their years together, Hartwig and Sedgman were by far the best middle-aged doubles team in the world. Hartwig's service return was consistently low and well placed, and Sedgman's was a thing of beauty. Taking serves deep in his backhand corner, Sedgman repeatedly skimmed the net with angled shots that made good volleys difficult. Yet he seldom hit a hard return and never a flat one that crossed the net shoulder high, inviting an easy putaway volley. Most often, Sedgman angled his returns toward the sideline, taking the volleyer wide and setting up a devastating follow-up shot down the middle.

Two strokes produce consistently low returns. One is a topspin drive, which sends the ball dipping once it has cleared the net. The second, most often hit off the backhand side, is the dink, a ball that's delicately undercut to slide softly over the net. The dink requires lots of touch to pull off, but it's worth developing if you play doubles seriously.

Try a lob return of serve. You might find it hard to believe, but the lob can make a highly effective service return. This is particularly true against teams that serve hard and volley well. Net rushers play close in, leaving themselves vulnerable to a ball that passes quickly over their heads. In addition, faced with a booming serve, you can get more control on a lob than on either a drive or a dink. The lob need not be perfect; anything that forces the attackers to retreat serves the purpose.

Turning the tables: Because the server is rushing forward and his partner is camped at the net, an offensive lob (right) can send them retreating to their own baseline.

You might lob, too, even if the server is staying at the baseline. It will give your team time to take a commanding net position.

Another timely use of the lob is when you are drawn wide to make a return. "Putting it up," as the saying goes, allows you to regain good position for the next shot. Finally, don't lob only at predictable times. Remember the value of the offensive lob: When you get a ball well inside the baseline and the netmen brace for a hard drive, flip a ball over them instead.

In short, it is hard to overwork the lob in senior doubles. Sedgman ruefully recalls a match many years ago in which his crafty opponents reversed the entire outcome with lobs. He was playing with fellow countryman Colin Long against two other outstanding Aussies, John Bromwitch and Adrian Quist. "We went up two sets and had 5-2, 40-15—two match points—on my serve," recalls Sedgman. "Then they hit a half dozen high lobs in a row. Long let 'em all bounce, which changed the rhythm of the game. They won every one of those points, and all of a sudden we were on the defensive. They beat us in five sets."

Hit directly at the poacher. What do you do if a poaching netman is giving you fits? You can't continue to return crosscourt; you'll try to hit too wide or too close to the net and wind up missing the shot. Hartwig and fellow Australian Lew Hoad demonstrated the proper antidote in a famous Davis Cup match in 1955. Americans Vic Seixas and Tony Trabert were bedeviling Hartwig and Hoad with poaches until the Aussies neutralized the tactic by hitting returns straight at or behind the moving netman. A less-decisive countermove to the poach, but still an effective one, is the lob. At the very least, it will buy time and prevent the opponents from controlling the point straightaway.

Foiling a poacher: One effective way to neutralize an ambitious, moving netman is to return down the line (right) behind him to catch him starting crosscourt.

Using Your Head to Win

Pay a visit to any bookstore these days and you're sure to find a number of books which address the topic of psychology in tennis. And, judging by the size of those books, you'd have to think that there's quite a bit to say on the subject.

Indeed, there certainly is. Tennis is a game that's played as much in the mind as on an actual tennis court. In fact, the world's top tennis players have been asserting that fact for years.

However, the purpose of this chapter is not so much to inform you of the latest theories in psychology and how they relate to tennis as it is to offer you a few ideas and suggestions about how you can use psychology to win more matches.

CONCENTRATE FOR A PSYCHOLOGICAL LIFT

How well do you concentrate in a match? Be honest. Few middle-aged players find it easy to block out thoughts of home, office, taxes, and hundreds of other daily concerns when they're on court. Yet concentration on the game is essential to good play.

So in a tough match requiring maximum concentration, try to deal with the smallest "unit" you can—the stroke you're about to hit. Don't worry about more distant objectives. By focusing all your attention on each stroke, you're in effect concentrating on game, set and match.

Such narrowly focused concentration gives you a big psychological advantage. It helps you avoid fretting over lost points, bad shots, and so on. We've probably all experienced frustration or dejection after blowing an easy shot and let the next few points slip away before we realize, or care, what's happening. You can

The look of concentration: By focusing all of your attention on each stroke like Sedgman (right), you're in effect concentrating on game, set and match.

avoid that kind of dangerous letdown by playing one point at a time and forgetting those that are already past.

YOUR INVISIBLE WEAPON

Psychology, of course, can also be used as a weapon. For senior players, the best psychological weapon is surprise. You can break your opponent's rhythm and jolt his expectations by changing tactics. Some of these moves were outlined in Chapter 5 on singles tactics: taking the net, perhaps behind the serve, to force the other fellow to hit a passing shot or a lob after he's been getting away with nothing but high, floating returns; serving as hard as you can, straight at him a time or two; and returning his serve with a lob, even if he's staying at the baseline. In short, keep him from taking you and your style of play for granted.

Another opportunity to use psychology and bolster your own prospects surfaces whenever you get tired in a long match. In these situations, do your damndest to keep the fact a secret. Don't drag your feet or shuffle around the court between points—the little energy you save won't compensate for the psychological damper you'll put on your spirits or the lift you'll give to your opponent's. Move briskly, or at least steadily, from deuce court to ad court during a game. Look composed and alert when you're changing sides and don't try to take more time than you're allowed for the changeover; that's not only unfair, it's a "dead" giveaway as to your physical condition.

Finally, a discussion of psychology and tennis wouldn't be complete without mentioning the small acts of "gamesmanship" that can influence the outcome

Psychology as a weapon: You can break your opponent's rhythm by changing tactics. Davidson (right) is a grand master at shifting gears to keep opponents honest.

of a match. In fact, senior tennis provides a perfect environment for these ploys as veterans seek to gain whatever edge they can over opponents in competitive events.

Perhaps the most common ploy is wearing all kinds of bandages and straps for ailments, both real and imagined. Things often reach the point where some fine senior players look like battlefield casualties when they step on the court.

Another gambit that's quite popular is to awe the opposition with a few anecdotal memories: the win over So-and-So at South Orange in '48; the near upset of the defending champion in the second round at Forest Hills, etc. Players don't do this on the court, of course, but at courtside, within earshot of their opponents, before the match.

And lastly, there's that proven maneuver—the carefully timed compliment. One outstanding senior has refined this to a devastating degree. When he's having a tough time returning one of his opponent's strokes, this fellow will sometimes start a conversation during the change of sides. He'll compliment the effectiveness of that stroke and perhaps ask for a demonstration—right there by the net post, maybe in slow motion. Then he waits for the guy to start thinking hard about what he's thus far been doing naturally. The result often is a deterioration of the stroke.

So savvy seniors, you see, know there are lots of ways out there to help win a match besides good shots. Whether or not you employ similar tactics, of course, is entirely up to you. But be aware that they do exist and are used quite extensively today. That way, perhaps, you'll be able to ignore them when you're played for a sucker.

Resorting to gamesmanship: To psyche out an opponent, some seniors will wear lots of bandages or outrageous clothing. Riggs (right) wrote the book on gamesmanship.

Conditioning Your Body to Perform

We've all seen aging, out-of-shape players hold their own on the court. It's almost as if they're playing on memory, stroking as they did when they were younger and moving instinctively, if laboriously, into proper position. If they were once good players, they can do that. The thing is, they can't do it for long.

Rex Hartwig summed up the situation neatly in a half-joking reference to himself at middle age: "I could always hit the ball all right. My problem is getting to it."

In the senior divisions, that's everyone's problem to a greater or lesser degree. And while the advance of age certainly can't be stopped, its effects can be diminished substantially if you adhere to a sound, sensible program of physical conditioning. Of course, there is no single fitness program that can or should be recommended for every middle-aged player. There are, however, a great assortment of exercises, training regimens and habits that can be selected from to find a suitable combination for each individual. The conditioning program you choose to follow depends on your personal tolerances and goals.

The Grand Masters, for example, really know themselves and their own bodies. When you're 25 and the coach says, "Run two miles and then do wind sprints every day," you can do that without questioning his order. But the Grand Masters have the attitude: "My body performs best when I do so and so." That seems to be characteristic of the good older athlete: He's always listening to ideas, but he doesn't automatically adopt them.

The important thing is that you establish *some* kind

The battle of the bulge: Riggs entered his famous match against Billie Jean King overweight and sluggish (right). He failed to make the necessary physical preparations.

of reasonably effective conditioning program. Without one, your prospects for success as a senior player and the satisfaction you derive from the sport will be severely restricted. Conditioning, you see, affects numerous aspects of your game. First, of course, it improves your stamina and ability to get to the ball. But a sound conditioning program will also sharpen your reflexes and quicken the speed with which you can recover from hitting one shot and prepare for the next.

For a graphic illustration of the price one pays for being out of shape, think back to Bobby Riggs' famous challenge match against Billie Jean King. Riggs was 55 at the time and, by his own admission, not in the best of physical condition. His easy victory over Margaret Court a year earlier had lulled him into overconfidence; he'd been beguiled by the mountains of publicity hailing him as the consummate male warrior in the "Battle of the Sexes." As a result, Riggs slacked off on his training and what he calls his "vitamin program." He came into the match overweight and sluggish.

To be sure, other factors contributed to his defeat—among them the fast court surface and King's aggressive and skillful play. But Riggs that day was his own toughest opponent. He sandbagged himself by failing to make the necessary physical preparations.

GENERAL FITNESS

Pancho Gonzalez has remarked that it takes twice as much effort to stay in shape at age 40 as it does at age 20. While we can't vouch for the scientific accuracy of that statement, there is no doubt that keeping fit in middle age is a much more demanding task.

Dr. James Nicholas, the New York City "sports doctor," outlines what the aging process does to "aerobic fitness," the body's ability to take in oxygen and pump it through an efficient heart: "From an aerobic standpoint, the peak of physical fitness comes between the

Conditioning problems: Gonzalez (right) believes that it takes twice as much effort to stay in shape at age 40 as it does at age 20.

ages of 18 and 25. In each subsequent decade, there is a drop in aerobic capacity. At 35, you've lost 10 to 15 percent of that age-25 capacity. At 55, the loss may be 20 percent or more."

The goal of a middle-age conditioning program, then, is not so much to "improve" fitness, but to retard its slippage. How does a senior player maintain his general physical fitness? For most of us, there are three possibilities: calisthenics, running, and playing tennis.

Few players rely on calisthenics alone to stay in shape, but it can be done. The bottom line here is you need to faithfully perform exercises that give your entire body a workout. Perhaps the best known and most effective are those found in the Royal Canadian Air Force exercise plans for men and women. Each program requires only about 12 minutes a day and leads the practitioner through gradually increasing "levels of performance" with the goal of improving flexibility, efficiency of the heart, and tone, strength, and endurance of muscles.

A common problem encountered in a calisthenics program, though, is boredom. So you might try singing songs as you exercise or reciting Shakespearean sonnets—anything to keep your mind active and alert. Do your entire fitness routine early in the morning, preferably as soon as you get out of bed. It's sure to wake you up and get your body's juices flowing after a restful night's sleep.

Running is a healthy supplement or alternative to calisthenics for senior players. It's a great way to stay in shape if you can't play more than a couple of times a week. However, don't equate running strictly with jogging. For this sport, which demands short, fast runs as well as endurance, running should include both jogging and sprinting.

So the general rule of thumb for tennis players is to jog long distances to promote stamina and overall fitness; sprint to increase speed and acceleration. How

Off and running: Emerson prepares his muscles for the short, rapid movements required on court by running wind sprints (right).

far should you jog? Far enough to feel as though you've had a real workout. How often? A couple of times a week, at least. Some high-level players—Torben Ulrich, for one—try to run every day that they don't play tennis.

Sprinting can be interwoven with jogging by accelerating a number of times during your run. You don't have to sprint far: 20 to 30 yards will suffice. And for maximum benefit, try sprinting sideways and backward as well. It will simulate two different aspects of court movement and improve your balance, too.

After three or four days of running, you should find you have more resiliency in your legs in a match. You'll get to more balls than you would have before and probably win a lot more points.

Finally, many players avoid calisthenics and running altogether. They believe that the only general conditioning one needs for tennis is tennis—lots of it.

If one can play *enough* tennis, the idea is probably sound. But "enough" might well mean six or seven sessions a week—singles, of course—and few people can spare that kind of time.

Even at the Grand Masters level, there have been, and still are, players who rely strictly on their play to keep them in shape. Hartwig, who retired in 1980, used to take that approach. Alex Olmedo and Whitney Reed take it today, along with occasional Grand Master Gardnar Mulloy, who is almost 20 years older than either of them, yet remains a model of senior conditioning.

"I'm a great believer in playing yourself into shape," Mulloy says. "Jogging? You don't jog on the court—why do it *for* the court? Anyway, jogging makes you lethargic."

Using your head: In a match, you'll have to turn your head often and quite quickly to follow the ball, so loosen your neck muscles as Davidson demonstrates (right).

Tom Brown, a Wimbledon and Forest Hills finalist who has played in some Grand Masters events, has deliberately increased his frequency of play as he's gotten older. "When I was younger," Brown says, "I found that I could play Wednesdays and Saturdays, say, and keep myself fit. In my 30s, maybe three times a week would do it. But in my 40s and now 50s, I like to speed it up to about four days a week."

Olmedo, when asked what he does for conditioning, shrugs and replies, "What *can* you do? Play tennis." That's what he did when he decided to join the Grand Masters after 17 years as a non-playing teaching pro. Now that he's once again in playing condition, Olmedo does a few calisthenics to loosen up for a match. "Mostly, though, I push myself as hard as I can on the court to keep my muscles tuned up," he says. "And I don't do any off-court running. Running is bad for your knees."

As for Reed, he treats conditioning as he treats life—with a light heart. "The game came so naturally to me," he says breezily, "I never had to sacrifice for it. I once went jogging a couple of days in a row and came down with a cold. At this point in my life, the hardest part of tennis is showing up for the match."

An interesting variation on playing yourself into shape is working yourself into it. Dodo Cheney, the perennial senior women's champion, tells us that's what she does around her house: "I've brought up three children and done the household duties that go with that. And I do a lot of yard work and gardening." Can that really be called conditioning? "You bet," she asserts. "I mean a *lot* of yard work, which involves constant stooping and stretching and especially bending your back. It's great for you."

PRE-MATCH STRETCHING ROUTINES

Whether you follow a calisthenics routine, run, or simply play matches, you should also do at least a few

Getting a leg up on an opponent: Before play begins, you should carefully limber up your leg muscles. Davidson shows how to stretch your upper legs on the right.

of the many kinds of stretching exercises that are beneficial to tennis players. Some of these exercises can be used in your regular conditioning program, but their primary function is to limber up your body before you begin play and put sudden demands on your muscles.

In middle age, when muscles, ligaments, and the like have lost some suppleness, it is almost essential that the player stretch immediately before stepping onto the court. If he doesn't, he runs a considerable risk of pulling muscles, tearing ligaments and suffering a number of other play-induced injuries. There are many ways to accomplish the task. Atlanta's Charlie Kidd, the come-lately senior champion, simply lies on his back with knees pulled up against his chest and his arms wrapped tightly around them. This position, he calculates, gradually stretches whatever body parts are likely to be suddenly stretched on the court.

Other stretching exercises include swinging your arms in a wide arc, doing knee bends and jumping-jacks, touching your toes, rotating your upper body at the waist and so forth. Any stretches that get your body parts moving slowly and regularly will do the job.

One part you should be sure to limber up is the Achilles tendon, which connects the heel with the calf muscle. It is particularly vulnerable to rupture, and such an injury can sideline the best of athletes for long periods. Sedgman, for example, "pulled" an Achilles in 1976 and was out for the rest of the season. His was a quick recovery. Any exercise that takes your weight forward while your heels are on the ground will stretch your Achilles. One is as simple as leaning against a fence or wall and slowly working your feet backward.

Arming yourself for play: Davidson (right) likes to loosen up his arms and shoulders by swinging them in circles.

Coming Back From Injuries and Layoffs

The human body contains roughly 600 joints, 500 to 600 muscles and 300 bones. Unfortunately, all of them present possible problems, especially for older players. A short list of common tennis injuries includes tendinitis of the shoulder, torn knee cartilage, recurring back pain, chronic pulled muscles (hamstring, thigh, and elbow) and "tennis toe," which sometimes results when the foot slides forward in a sudden stop and slams against the front of the shoe.

The arm, wrist, shoulder and knees are especially vulnerable because tennis requires a lot of arm movement and stop-and-go footwork. "People who are not strong and flexible in the joints run the risk of injury," says Dr. James Nicholas, "but they often fail to recognize the incipient signs. And people who've had athletic-type injuries before—and by 35 or 45, almost every active person has—are prone to get them again."

That, of course, is no reason to avoid playing tennis. It is simply a reason to be prudent in assessing your physical condition, in warming up, in playing within your limits.

"Tennis elbow" is the malady most commonly associated with the sport, although it can be the result of other activities such as throwing a baseball or even painting a wall. It is certainly tennis' most talked about and most vexing injury.

What is tennis elbow? According to Dr. Nicholas, the genesis of the injury is a disintegration of the "Sharpey's fibers," strands of connective tissue that attach bone to muscle at the elbow. And usually, tennis elbow is the result of improper stroking form which puts an excessive amount of stress on these tissues.

Like many other diagnosticians, Dr. Nicholas feels that a lengthy layoff is the best medicine "*if* you avoid straining the elbow altogether. That means no lifting luggage with the racquet hand, no gripping the steering wheel so tightly you produce strain."

Are there other remedies? "Anything that substantially increases the supply of blood to the injured area," Dr. Nicholas says. "The methods would

3 EXERCISES TO HELP PREVENT TENNIS ELBOW

1. To strengthen your wrist and forearm, do the wrist curl exercise shown above. Using a 5-pound weight, begin doing five to 10 repetitions twice a day. Gradually build up to 20 to 25 repetitions three times daily. For lateral tennis elbow, hold the dumbbell with your palm facing up. For medial tennis elbow, hold the weight with your palm down.

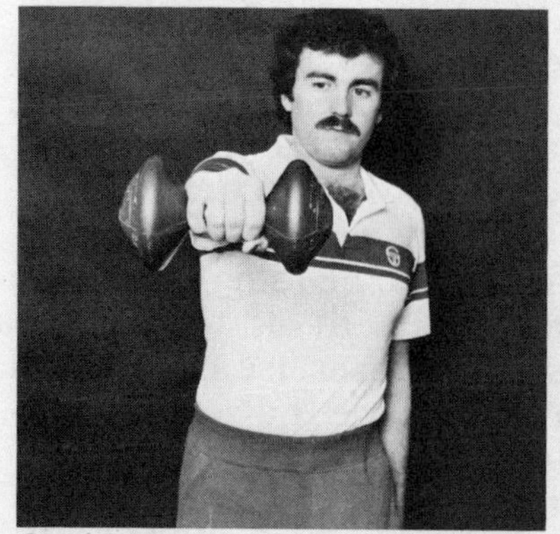

2. To build up your shoulder muscles, raise a dumbbell slowly from below your waist to shoulder height. Repeat the exercise five times straight ahead (as shown in the photo), then five times sideways.

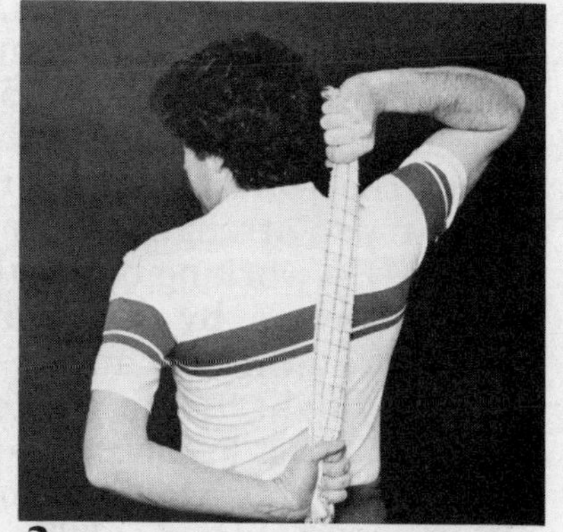

3. To stretch your shoulder and upper arm muscles before exercising or playing, hold a towel behind your back, as shown in the photo, and gently pull in both directions for a count of five. Repeat three times.

include acupuncture, heat, and rubbing the spot firmly with your finger. None of these, however, will produce better than about a 60 percent cure." Very few tennis elbows, he adds, require surgery or benefit from it.

A change in racquets might also provide some relief in the long run. Stiff frames, for example, typically transmit more ball-impact shock up the arm to the elbow than more flexible frames. So a switch of racquets—from stiff to flexible, from heavy to light or vice versa—could take the stress off the inflamed part of your elbow and place it on a healthy area instead.

But after an elbow-induced layoff, Dr. Nicholas says, a player's best bet is to "cast aside a faulty stroke and learn the proper one. He's in the same situation that faced Nolan Ryan as a major-league baseball pitcher. Ryan threw overarm until he developed pain. Now he throws three-quarter arm."

In short, recovery from all tennis injuries, not just tennis elbow, requires sensible treatment. It demands a thorough resting of the affected muscles or joints to minimize the danger of reinjury, bearing in mind that healing of this sort takes longer with advancing age.

Strengthening exercises, too, often play a major role in affecting a player's comeback. Torben Ulrich nursed an ailing knee for some 15 years before getting a diagnosis of torn "miniscus" cartilage. He immediately embarked on an exercise rehabilitation program.

"I try to strengthen it in all kinds of ways," Ulrich says. "By working out with weights, bending backward and sideways, by wading in a pool with old tennis shoes on, by rotating the ankles so that I exercise the knee as well, by light jumping on a trampoline. I also use an instrument a French doctor gave me—a kind of platform that tips back and forth on two half tennis balls. You need to react quickly on it to keep your balance." He believes his little regimen has forestalled an operation while permitting him to cavort as the most agile of middle-aged athletes.

REMARKABLE COMEBACKS

At least two more Grand Masters, Frank Parker and Sven Davidson, have made remarkable recoveries from

Rehabilitation work: Ulrich stretches to strengthen his knee.

injury. Parker, who was twice the champion at Forest Hills, suffered a herniated disc at age 56 that had some doctors convinced he wouldn't walk again. "I couldn't even lift a cup of coffee," he remembers now. Told that surgery would either make him well or make him a cripple with the odds about even, he took the gamble and won. Now in his mid-60s, Parker still plays excellent weekend tennis.

Miraculous is a more suitable term to describe Davidson's recovery. The "injury" in his case was a pair of coronary attacks that required a five-bypass, open-heart operation.

In July 1980, while carrying his luggage through a railway station in his native Sweden (he now lives in California), Davidson suddenly lost consciousness and collapsed. Passersby administered mouth-to-mouth resuscitation, and doctors at the hospital injected adrenalin and gave him four electric shocks. The diagnosis: a viral infection of the heart. Several weeks later, he was back on the Grand Masters circuit, feeling tired, not winning regularly, but playing hard.

Then, in mid-January of 1981, at a practice tournament in Los Angeles, he lunged for a passing shot and slumped to the court, regaining consciousness just long enough to ask for an ambulance. Again, bystanders kept him alive until paramedics arrived to deliver, this time right at the scene, electric shocks and adrenalin. Using a catheter probe, doctors detected "plaque" at five points in the coronary arteries. To continue even a quiet life, open-heart surgery was necessary.

But Davidson had no interest in leading a quiet life. Less than two months after the surgery, he was hitting balls on his southern California court. And although a return to tournament competition seemed impossible, he told his doctors that was exactly what he wanted to do. "One doctor told me not to be too optimistic," he

Miraculous recovery: Two months after open-heart surgery, Davidson (right) was back on the court hitting balls.

says. "But that doctor called a renowned colleague in Seattle, who said, 'Tell him to play to his heart's delight.' "

The clever pun was a welcome sign for Davidson because it meant he could resume his professional career. And in May, slightly less than four months after his quintuple bypass, he took the court against Alex Olmedo in a first-round match. "Alex," he recalls, "was kind enough to give me five games."

COMING BACK AFTER A LAYOFF

Few players ever have to deal with medical problems as immense as Davidson's. Yet his comeback should serve as an inspiration to all of us. Suppose you were recuperating from an injury or a long illness . . . or perhaps just dusting off the cobwebs from an inactive winter season. How would you get back into the swing of things on court?

First and foremost, as a senior player, you should work yourself into playing shape gradually so as to avoid putting undue strain on your muscles and heart. If you've noticed any significant change in your physical condition since the preceding season, a visit to your doctor is in order for a medical exam, plus a discussion of your proposed tennis program.

Assuming you get the go-ahead, start a program of limbering-up exercises at least a couple of weeks before taking to the court. Supplement the program with the kind of running—jogging combined with sprints—discussed in the last chapter. If you're coming off a period of general inactivity, you might want to begin the running on a track or some other soft surface to avoid jarring sensitive areas in the legs. A golf course would be an excellent place to start.

If you intensely dislike having to gradually work your way into shape after layoffs, you ought to consider starting a year-round fitness program. Dr. Nicholas urges a two-pronged program geared to middle-aged players. The first part, promoting general fitness, involves 20 to 40 minutes of exercise per day, three or four days a week: bicycling, running, dancing, as well as tennis. Part two is geared toward increasing "flexibility," which, Dr. Nicholas points out, diminishes with age and is in short supply in some people to begin with.

"If you're innately stiff," he says, "you need to work much harder than the person who can put his palms on the floor while keeping his legs straight. You need long warm-ups with lots of stretching and two to four minutes worth of rhythmic movement of arms and legs to make the heart pump vigorously."

Among the Grand Masters, Davidson follows the most elaborate fitness regimen. He bases it on running and limbering-up exercises. "The key thing in tennis is really who's best at getting to the ball," the Swede explains. "That's why I try to run 30 minutes every day—variously sprinting, running and walking. And I try to do it first thing in the morning. Otherwise, I can think of 300 reasons why I *shouldn't* run."

In addition to a fitness regimen, a good diet will help you ease into an active court life. Unfortunately, when it comes to food and drink and how much of each to consume, the demands of conditioning run up against strong, and sometimes unbreakable, bad habits.

You should be guided by two considerations in making a comeback: how serious you are about the sport (that is, whether or not you want to play tournaments regularly); and how willing you are to give up off-court pleasures. Obviously, it makes little sense to embark on any serious comeback attempt while consuming great quantities of liquor or fattening food. Smoking, of course, won't help you either. Beyond that, let your objectives, and your willpower, be your guide.

C. Alphonso Smith reports that surprising numbers of participants in the Super Senior tournaments are serious abstainers from the wrong kinds of food and drink. Their attitude toward maintaining a healthy diet seems to pervade various levels of the typical middle-aged player's game today.

Getting Better As You Get Older

Middle-aged players often take a lackadaisical attitude toward their games. "Why should I worry?" they seem to be saying. "I'm just happy to be able to play and enjoy myself." Certainly, there's nothing wrong with that attitude. In fact, one of the beauties of tennis is that it can be played on a variety of levels.

We assume, however, that you probably want to play better tennis than you currently do. Perhaps you'll be able to take our suggestions and incorporate them directly into your present games without much difficulty. Chances are, though, you'll have to work to strengthen your game. And that work will entail a certain amount of practice and, perhaps, professional lessons. How much practice and how many lessons will depend primarily on your answers to the two basic questions presented in Chapter Two: What kind of player are you and what kind do you want to be?

Bill Tilden's drive was focused on one goal—to be the best tennis player in the world. Early in his career, Tilden took an entire winter off so he could practice indoors in Providence, R.I., to strengthen a weak backhand. He brought in less-accomplished players and told them to work over his backhand in practice matches. Tilden lost to those players repeatedly, but when he left Providence to resume his tournament career, he had a backhand that would take him to the top.

Of course, that type of inner desire is exceptionally rare at any level of play. In your group of senior players, you probably will even find it tough to locate partners who want to practice in a careful, sustained manner. Some may be willing to extend the normal

Fierce determination (right): Tilden's drive was focused on one goal—to be the best tennis player in the world.

warm-up before starting a set, but the idea of practicing any longer may strike them as a terrible misuse of valuable playing time.

In areas of the country where court time is hard to get, that attitude is understandable. However, it certainly doesn't promote improvement. In this game, you have to put in your time on a practice court to raise your level of play.

USE PRACTICE TIME WISELY

Let's say you're eager to improve and willing to practice, but you can't find a partner who shares your ambition. How can you work on your strokes?

For solo practice sessions, the only partner you need is a sturdy backboard. Many clubs and public playing facilities have backboards and there's seldom a charge for using them. But if you're fortunate enough to have a court in your own backyard, you might consider installing a backboard because it won't cost you a great deal of money. Another perfectly suitable option is to locate a building in your area that has a windowless concrete wall away from automobile traffic. There, you can practice until your heart's content.

When hitting against a backboard, there are two areas you'll want to work on: stroke production and footwork. Each requires different practice techniques.

To work on your strokes, stand back far enough from the board or wall so you won't be rushed in hitting the ball as it rebounds. Your objective is to execute your stroke properly, from backswing to follow-through. Don't dash after balls to hit them on one bounce. Instead, let the ball bounce two or three times, if necessary, so you can get your racquet back early and swing smoothly. Try to hit *every* ball with the proper stroke—one you've been taught in a lesson or learned from a book.

When you first work on that stroke, don't attempt to do much hitting on the run. Instead, simply catch balls that rebound more than a couple of steps from where you're standing. After you learn to stroke with control in a stationary position, you can hit balls that rebound on an angle to force you to move and hit on the run as you do in actual play.

To improve footwork and reflexes, hit the ball on only *one* bounce. Now your purpose is to run down balls and keep your balance as you make smooth strokes. This footwork exercise, as you can imagine, will tire you quickly. You may want to alternate five minutes of this practice routine with 10 minutes of the multiple-bounce stroking exercise. Incidentally, you can include volleying in each exercise by moving closer to the board and hitting the ball before it bounces on the ground. We recommend that you use relatively dead balls for this drill so they won't bounce back so fast.

For obvious reasons, solo practicing on a full court is pretty much restricted to serving. However, it's a great way to groove your service motion. When you can find an empty court, first lay down a couple of targets—a ball can and racquet cover, for example—in the back corners of a service court. Then, practice a smooth service motion, aiming for your targets. See how close you can come to hitting them.

Of course, while solo serving practice and backboard drills can work wonders for your game, there's no substitute for putting your strokes to the true test on court by hitting with a practice partner—someone who'll not only rally with you, but rally with a specific purpose.

For example, maybe both of you would like to work on your crosscourt forehands. If that's the case, start a crosscourt rally hitting nothing but forehands and try to keep the ball in play for as long as possible. And later, if he wants to practice his service returns, you can refine your serving motion.

As you can see, such practice sessions can be mutually beneficial. The knock against them, many players say, is that they're boring. To prevent your workouts from becoming dull, you can devise some impromptu games to keep your interests and your spirit alive. For instance, you might draw a chalk line across the court, halfway between the service lines and baselines, and declare that balls falling short of the line (as well as beyond the baseline) count as a point against the hitter. You'll be surprised to see how many more balls begin to fall into the prescribed area after you introduce this type of challenge to your workouts.

Playing practice sets can be both fun and beneficial for your game, provided you don't lapse into your poor stroking form just to get the ball over the net and win a point. Hit the "right" way, even if it costs you that point. Otherwise, you'll be undercutting your own learning process and reinforcing the very habits you're trying to break.

If strokes aren't your major concern, use practice sets to work on tactics. Are your approach shots weak? Do you have difficulty putting away your overheads? If so, go to the net at every decent opportunity. Hit deep approach shots to the corners and, if your opponent lobs, try to angle off the overhead for a winner. If you have trouble playing the seniors' standard backcourt game, then stay back and rally. Keep returning the ball several feet over the net. Don't worry if you hit some balls over the baseline; just get the feel of hitting deep. In short, make a practice set just what the name implies—practice, without concern over who wins or loses.

Do you want to try a real practice regimen? Do you have a friend, at your level of play who wants one too? Then you might consider the system devised by Horace Proulx, a southern Californian who took up tennis at age 46 and, several years later, earned a national senior ranking.

"My secret is to hit lots of tennis balls," Proulx says, "5,000 of them per week. No less." The determined senior breaks down his practice time into four 90-minute sessions every seven days. If you follow his training schedule, he continues, "At the end of three months, you will have hit about 65,000 tennis balls. I know it sounds exhausting. But you will have no trouble doing it, and it's fun. By the end of this time, your game will have improved to a level you did not believe possible. In six months, your skills will have reached another plateau."

Of course, it's not necessary to immerse yourself in such a time-consuming, energy-sapping schedule to see improvement in your game. But every little bit of practice time you can get is sure to help you become more effective on court.

Professional help: Seixas demonstrates good serving form.

SEEK PROFESSIONAL ASSISTANCE

Whether you're a weekend hacker or an accomplished tournament veteran, a couple of sessions with a local teaching professional can pay big dividends in terms of increasing the amount of enjoyment you get out of playing the sport.

For the senior neophyte or near-neophyte, of course, the advantages of professional instruction are obvious: He learns the proper methods of stroking the ball, reduces the risk of injury and has a fun-filled time on court. Players who try to teach themselves, on the other hand, usually wind up with strange stroking motions that lead to injury and develop bad habits that are extremely difficult to break later in life.

If you're set in your tennis ways but want to change them, you'd better allow many hours and a fair amount of money to reach your goal. For a while, you may have to stop playing for fun in order to use your court time to practice the new strokes you're trying to learn. Gradually work your way into easy, no-pressure matches, hitting those strokes—the right way only—at every opportunity. If you then find yourself lapsing back into your old swing, go back to practicing until you're confident the new one is grooved. That may sound like a stiff price to pay for improving your game, but if you're shopping for basic improvements, you'll have to pay it.

Advanced players, too, can get some helpful stroking and tactical advice by rallying occasionally with a pro. Even the superstars of the game sometimes find odd little gremlins creeping into their form and weakening their overall effectiveness. They work with expert coaches to repair the chinks in their armor; why shouldn't experienced, amateur senior players, as well?

How do you find a pro to whom you can entrust your game? First of all, look for an instructor who is a certified member of the United States Professional Tennis Association or the Professional Tennis Registry. These pros must pass extensive written and on-court examinations to earn certification, so they should know their business.

Beyond that, your best bet is to visit tennis clubs in your area and talk with their members; they're sure to have favorite pros. In fact, they'll probably be able to tell you which pros work best with social players and which relish the thought of putting tournament players through tough practice drills.

When you finally locate a pro who is able to work wonders with your strokes, stick with him. He's like a good mechanic; he'll keep your game running smoothly.

CHECK OUT THE LATEST EQUIPMENT

Not so long ago, choosing equipment was the simplest aspect of tennis. There were perhaps a half-dozen popular racquets, plus a few exotic imported models available, all of them made of wood and all with a hitting surface of standard shape and size. Strings were either nylon or gut, and there weren't many kinds of each. Naturally, you had your racquet strung with gut if you were good, affluent, pretentious, or all of the above. Few manufacturers offered "lines" of tennis clothes. Dressing appropriately meant wearing cotton shorts, cotton shirt and possibly a tennis sweater—all white save, perhaps, a couple of discreet bands of color on the sweater.

We needn't spell out how drastically all that has changed. What was once the simplest part of the sport now has become the most complicated. Racquet choices often involve making agonizing decisions, as well as major investments. Tennis shirts and shorts are now part of multi-hued, designer-label "ensembles," and many of them are covered by flashy, satin-like warm-up suits. Even the old tennis sneaker—the trusty Converse or Jack Purcell—has metamorphosed and turned into the composite-soled, nylon-mesh "tennis shoe."

What follows is a brief guided tour along the main paths of a dense forest filled with tennis equipment.

RACQUETS

The oversized racquet (Prince, et al) is, in many experts' opinion, the most important breakthrough in tennis since Maurice McLoughlin introduced net-rushing some 60-odd years ago. Even world-class players in the open division have taken to the large frames with remarkable enthusiasm. And among seniors, the "big head" now clearly dominates the market. C. Alphonso Smith estimates that 85 percent of senior men play with an oversized model, including all but a couple of the Grand Masters themselves.

Converts to the oversized-racquet revolution claim there are a number of advantages afforded by the big weapons. Most important, they say, is the larger "sweetspot" (the most responsive area of strings) these frames offer. Thus, the argument goes, fewer weak shots are caused by off-center hits. The racquets also are said to produce more power and afford more control than conventional frames.

But not everyone is convinced. After experimenting with a Prince racquet a few years ago, Sven Davidson says he found the frame "bad . . . too wobbly. I don't believe the big racquet has anything on the standard version, except a marvelous sales pitch." Not even a larger sweetspot? "That's B.S.," he continued. "You still have to hit the ball at or near the center. Otherwise, it will twist in your hand. I think the oversized is a fad that will eventually die out."

Remarkable changes: Today's racquets (far right) are bigger and stronger than those of yesteryear (near right).

Alex Olmedo, who also swears by his standard racquet, cites a common complaint against the big ones—a "trampolining" effect, in which the racquet's longer strings "give" at impact with the ball and tend to propel it farther than intended. Olmedo can't see how anybody can claim control as an attribute of oversized frames: "I don't get as much control with it, and all my tennis life, control's been the thing to aim for."

Current buying trends refute these objections, however. Along with other age groups, seniors find that the larger racquet heads simply give you more margin for error on the stroke.

Midsized frames have also become quite popular in the last couple of years because they combine the desirable features of both "extremes" in racquet size. Among the Grand Masters, Frank Sedgman, Neale Fraser, and Gardnar Mulloy all use a midsized model. (Mulloy notes that he urged Spalding to make a large-headed racquet 20 years ago and that, "before World War II, *all* heads were a little larger than today's standard.")

While racquet head size is a controversial topic these days, so, too, is racquet *weight* and *grip size*. One school of thought contends that both should decrease as you get older, in recognition of the fact that seniors don't have as much strength as they used to in their arms and hands. But according to an opposing theory, a heavier racquet—especially one that's heavier in the head—does more of the work at impact. Thus, many senior players apparently would be better off with a medium-weight frame.

How do you decide what size and weight racquet to use? Because a racquet's "feel" is such a subjective matter, a serious player is foolish to buy any of them without making comparisons. So borrow a friend's racquet for a set or two—you'll need that long to get the real feel of it—or find a tennis shop that loans "demonstrator" racquets. The manager won't let you take out everything in the shop, of course, and he'll expect you to buy a frame eventually. What's more, you'll probably pay more there than at a high-volume discount store, but you'll be certain that what you're getting suits you.

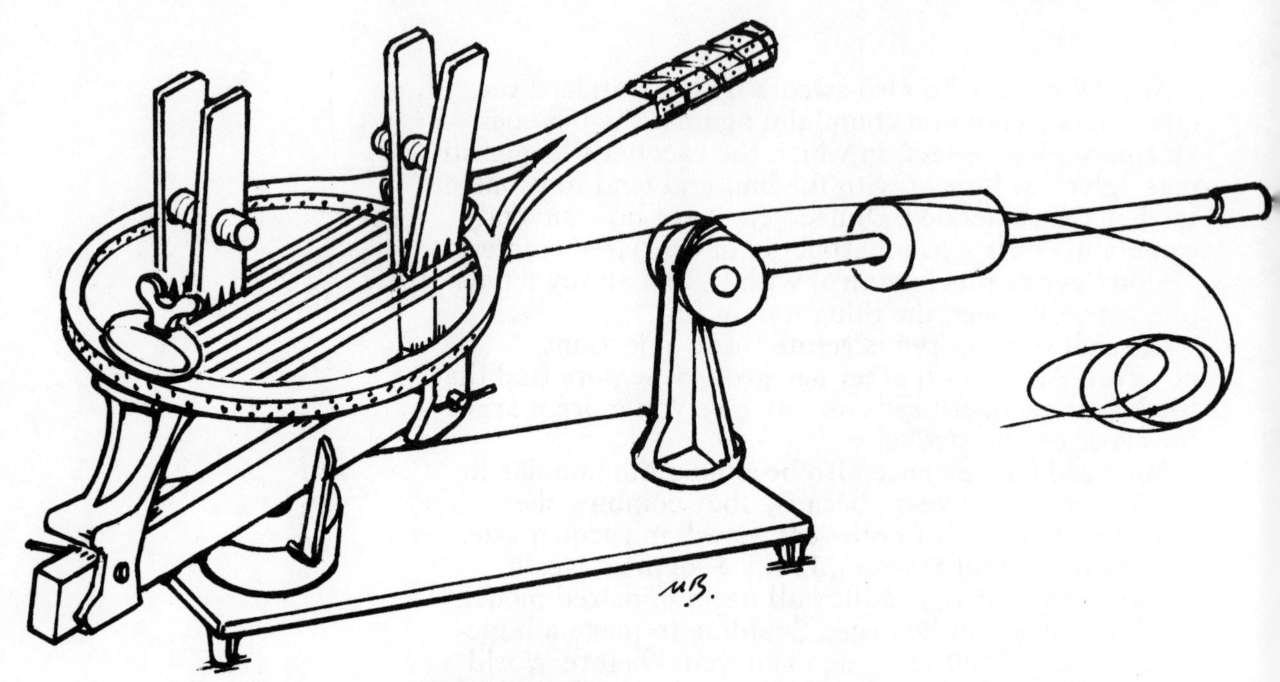

STRINGING

Stringing decisions: To select a type of string and tension, consider your style of play and skill level.

String tensions vary even more widely than racquet models, from Bjorn Borg's 80-odd pounds per square inch to the 20-pounds-per-square-inch "fishnet" used by Italian Beppe Merlo, another former Grand Master. Generally, though, for a standard-sized frame, you should try a string tension of 45 to 55 pounds. For an oversized frame, you should increase that tension by about 20 pounds (about 10 for a midsized model) to avoid the powerful trampolining effect mentioned earlier.

Now, the question arises: What type of string should you use—gut or nylon? To answer it wisely, you should become familiar with the performance characteristics of each.

In brief, natural gut provides a better feel than nylon and for that reason, is preferred by most tournament players. It's also quite expensive and wears out more quickly. Nylon, in contrast, is not as responsive as natural gut, but the difference in performance usually is too subtle for the average player to notice. It wears very well, even at high string tensions required by large-headed racquets, and costs less than its natural counterpart.

As with racquet preference, your choice between gut and nylon string is a personal, subjective one. You should make a decision based on your playing ability, style of play and, of course, the state of your finances.

FOOTWEAR

At last count, more than 200 models of quality tennis shoes were being sold on the market. This footwear has evolved substantially in recent years because of research performed in the wake of the running boom in this country. As a result, today's tennis shoes are lighter, more flexible, supportive and comfortable than models available just a few short years ago.

You, of course, are the beneficiary of all these improvements. Don't be afraid to experiment a little. Try a pair of shoes, for example, that features a nylon-mesh upper. This material is exceptionally light and cool around your feet. You might find you can stay on court longer, wearing them instead of your heavy leather "hiking boots." Look into different tread patterns, too. If you play mostly on soft, granular surfaces, a herringbone pattern will minimize slippage; if you prefer hard-court play, a nubbed tread will provide better traction.

Comfort and performance: Experiment to find the tennis shoe that's right for you.

Testing the Tournament Waters

Are you satisfied with your tennis development? Would you like to get a better idea of how your game stacks up against those of other senior players in your city, your state. . . perhaps even the country? If so, you can put your competitive mettle to a true test by entering the world of organized tournaments.

Before you take the big step, though, you should be aware that the tournament game is going to put some pretty tough demands on you. It's not at all like heading out to your country club on a sunny afternoon to have some fun on court with friends. Players in tournaments tend to take things pretty seriously once the first ball is served in a match. And if you're not prepared to deal with that type of attitude, you may be wasting your time.

Let's take a look at how you can make your first tournament experience a rewarding one.

MATCH PREPARATION

If you're a newcomer to the tournament scene, you'll be tempted to pore over the draw sheet and worry about meeting specific opponents if you get by the early rounds. But you should follow the example set by Don Budge, who won a long, long string of tournaments in his competitive lifetime: "I never looked at the draw because I didn't care who I played. Each round was to be dealt with as it came. Otherwise, sure enough somebody would knock me off."

The first step in making that attitude pay off for you in a tournament is to carefully evaluate each opponent you face. What are his strengths and weaknesses? Is he in shape to hang in there on a long point? To cover repeated drop shots? Talk to friends who've played the fellow, and, if you have the opportunity, watch him

Budge (right) on tournament play: "I never looked at the draw because I didn't care who I played. Each round was to be dealt with as it came."

play. Nobody will think you're a spy or intruder; sizing up the opposition is a basic, and honorable, part of the game.

Obviously, you should also get plenty of rest before the tournament starts and as much between matches as you can. As a senior, you'll need more recovery time. That means a good night's sleep and maybe an afternoon nap if you have one match in the morning and another in the late afternoon.

If you're anticipating a long match, use common sense in practicing or jogging the day before so you don't wear yourself out. Limit the practice to a single set or a good hitting session. In either case, don't work on new strokes or shots. It's too late for that. If you haven't brought your game to the tournament, you won't find it when you're down 0-5 in the third.

Pre-match eating and drinking is largely a matter of personal habit and metabolism. But, obviously, you won't want to eat heavily or drink an appreciable amount of alcohol. In his glory days, Rex Hartwig recalls, "I could go and have a big T-bone steak and then race out to play five sets. If I did that now, I'm sure I'd die. Now I don't eat for quite a few hours beforehand, and when I do, it'll only be a sandwich or a large salad."

When the weather is hot, make sure your tennis clothing is absorbent and lightweight. Remember, too, that white is "cooler" than darker colors in direct sun. Bring a few wristbands, a large towel to use when changing sides, and perhaps a small towel to tuck into your shorts. A hat or visor can come in handy, too, when playing in bright sunlight. And finally, unless water is provided at courtside, take along whatever you'll want to drink.

As for racquets, always come with more than one, even if your spare frames aren't your favorites. Nothing is so enraging in a tight match as breaking a string and having to play with an unfamiliar, borrowed model. If you should enter more than an occasional tournament, you should invest in a duplicate or two of your favorite racquet. And make sure it *is* a duplicate in all respects.

At some large tournaments, court time is at a premium. So when you get an opportunity to warm up on

Wise warm-up: Olmedo loosens up for play.

another court before your match, by all means take it. Pre-match warm-up techniques vary considerably, even within the small Grand Masters troupe. For example, Sven Davidson goes through a calisthenics routine and then hits ground strokes for about a half hour from well behind the baseline. "I develop a good feel for the ball," Davidson explains, "and standing far back helps that, as well as helps me to watch the ball closely. Once I have done those things, I think I'm ready to play any place on the court."

The warm-ups used by Frank Sedgman and Neale Fraser, on the other hand, differ considerably from Davidson's as well as from each other's. Sedgman likes to be alone on court, hitting serves 15 or 20 minutes; he says he finds his rhythm and loosens up his muscles that way. Fraser prefers a "light" rally, just enough to make him "a quicker starter" in the match. "Too many people use the first few games as a warm-up period, instead of getting a jump on the opponent," he contends.

MATCH PLAY

When warming up with your opponent immediately before the match, practice of any kind should be the furthest thing from your mind. You should concentrate on acclimating yourself to the conditions at hand—the court surface, background, position of the sun, and so forth—as well as on getting a feel for your opponent's game.

You should also be limbering up. Run around, bend your knees and hit smooth, flowing ground strokes. Don't worry about pace or precise placement, simply establish your rhythm. Make sure you hit at least a few of every stroke. Take 10 or 12 practice serves if you feel you need them; hit some to the ad as well as the deuce court.

Should you elect to serve first if you win the racquet spin? That depends. Some players believe that if you get the opportunity to take the offensive, you should seize it. Should you win the first game and the set proceeds "on serve" (no service breaks), your opponent will always be under the gun, knowing that losing his serve can mean the loss of the set.

However, there's another argument that seems slightly more convincing, especially at the senior level. It is based on the idea that, in the first game, your opponent will still be somewhat stiff and nervous and that if you let him serve first, you'll stand a good chance of breaking him immediately. Naturally, while he's serving that first game, you'll have an extra few minutes to limber up before you have to hit your own deliveries. If you do elect to receive, play your returns on the safe side, letting him make errors while you find the tennis equivalent of your "sea legs."

What should you do if you meet a younger player who hits much harder than you? First, you should recognize the hopelessness of trying to match his power, stroke for stroke. The advantage you may have over him is steadiness, experience and above all, patience. Try to keep him moving and guessing, and don't go for many winners yourself. Take even more pace off your shots. Feed him enough balls, especially enough *different kinds* of balls (spins, lobs, etc.), and the chances are he'll begin to miss.

As a senior, one of your most important considerations in a tournament match is to conserve energy, so take the maximum time allowed between points and games. And how hard you scramble for a point or a game should depend on the score. If you're down love-40, unless it's triple match point, don't try to run down an almost-certain putaway. Save yourself. You'll live to play another day.

Conversely, if you're winning and your opponent shows signs of tiring, don't let him stall. There are time limits for various match-play situations. If necessary, ask for an umpire to be assigned to your match, and see that he enforces them. Remember that time and rest are vital factors in senior competition. Don't let an opponent exploit them unfairly.

So there are a few guidelines you can follow to help ease your way into the tournament game. Whatever your results, try to treat each match as a learning experience and benefit from it.

Always keep in mind the phrase: "You're not getting older, you're getting better." In a very special way, you're a Grand Master, too.